The Dance in America

the text of this book is printed
on 100% recycled paper

THE DANCE

NEW YORK · EVANSTON · SAN FRANCISCO · LONDON

Walter Terry
IN AMERICA

revised edition

HARPER COLOPHON BOOKS
Harper & Row, Publishers

Originally published in a hardcover edition by
Harper & Row, Publishers.

THE DANCE IN AMERICA, Revised Edition.
Copyright © 1956, 1971 by Walter M. Terry, Jr.
All rights reserved. Printed in the United States of America. No part
of this book may be used or reproduced in any manner without written
permission except in the case of brief quotations embodied in critical
articles and reviews. For information address Harper & Row, Publishers, Inc., 10 East 53rd Street, New York, N.Y. 10022. Published
simultaneously in Canada by Fitzhenry & Whiteside Limited, Toronto.

First HARPER COLOPHON edition published 1973

STANDARD BOOK NUMBER: 06–090313–9

For Phoebe Barr

Contents

Illustrations

The following pictures appear in a group after page 178

Illustrations

Acknowledgment

Because modern dance in America was the result of rebellion by individuals against schools of dance and dance conventions, its story has been told here mainly in terms of dance biography, in a relating of the characteristics, drives, concepts and achievements of those who spearheaded the modern-dance movement in our land.

I am deeply grateful to the late Ruth St. Denis, Doris Humphrey and Helen Tamiris, and to Ted Shawn, Martha Graham and Hanya Holm for giving me hours of their time and sharing with me many of their profoundest dance thoughts in helping me assemble the very special material contained in those chapters treating with their unique contributions to dance in America.

Part I

The Heritage

I

Dance Landscape

Dancing, to the first Americans, was a necessity. It was not a sin, as it was to certain of the first white settlers, nor was it merely a pleasant diversion, as it is to the majority of contemporary Americans. It was more than universally popular, more than culturally important. It was an essential ingredient of life itself.

The American Indian, like his primitive brothers in all quarters of the globe, would have had no difficulty understanding what the great English philosopher Havelock Ellis meant when he said, in his *The Dance of Life,* "If we are indifferent to the art of dancing, we have failed to understand, not merely the supreme manifestation of physical life, but also the supreme symbol of spiritual life." For the American Indian could not and would not divorce dancing from worship, from love, from enmity, from the growing of crops, from the hunt, from fertility, from death and from rebirth. He knew that dance made magic.

The white man's dance heritage, except for the most ancient of days, was wholly different. He would, perhaps, quite willingly accept the definition of ballet (one of the many forms of dance) set down in the sixteenth century by Balthazar de Beaujoyeulx, who staged the first ballet, *Le Ballet Comique de la Reine,* for the Queen of France. To Beaujoyeulx, ballet was "a geometrical arrangement of numerous people dancing together under a diverse harmony of many instruments."

America's dance, which is perhaps the richest and which is certainly the most varied in the world, invites a public response which ranges from rejection through mild indifference to pleased acceptance and devotion.

To a few Americans, the art of dance is a necessity; to an increasing number, it is as important and as stimulating as the arts of music, drama, literature or painting; and to millions, it is a new and exciting form of entertainment.

What is dance? Between the two poles of "a necessity" and "a diversion" lie the many functions of dance, the many services (some great and some small) which it can perform. At its most popular level in America, it serves as a form of social recreation. In a highly modified version of ancient nuptial or courtship dances, men and women, boys and girls dance together in male-female pairs to the popular music of the day. With bodies held close and hands touching, they enjoyed (until the separate-but-equal dance style came into being) a rhythmic union socially acceptable to all but a few antidance sects or individuals.

In jitterbugging, where the courtship element was at a minimum, stress was placed upon the channeling of youthful (and sometimes excessive) energy into rhythmic form. This also represented an ancient dance purpose, for humans since the beginning of time have enjoyed expending energies, physical and emotional, in formal rhythms.

With many folk-dance forms, the couple dance gives way to group participation. Contacts with neighbors and friends and even newcomers to the community are arranged through formal designs executed in prescribed rhythms.

All of these are recreational dances, although most of them have their half-forgotten roots in dances of magic of the distant past. They are enjoyable, even important, but no one maintains that they illumine the spirit, stir the mind to profound thoughts or lift the soul in religious ecstasy. Such is not their purpose.

Then there are those dance materials used for education, movements which develop the muscles of the body, enhance coordination, create balance. Used therapeutically, dance exercises, dance rhythms can aid in the restoring of injured bodies and broken minds. Here is dance as a discipline.

In social, folk and educational dances, the individual is a doer, a participant. In the theater of dance, the individual, unless he is the performer, becomes a watcher, a nonparticipant in the physical sense but a participant in an art experience.

On its simplest level, theatrical dancing is concerned with entertainment, with easy diversion. As the average tap dancer performs, the onlooker commences to forget his problems, his worries or even his own boredom. Rhythms of tapping feet invite attention, and the good nature, sensuousness, coquetry or speed of the dancer steal one's thoughts away from minor cares.

Vicariously, the watcher experiences the fun of dancing and, perhaps, even identifies his own untrained body with the light and dexterous body of the dancer. Certainly, in exhibition ballroom dancing, identification was even closer, for the performers took a kind of dancing which belongs to everyone and through little enhancements and more spectacular embellishments lifted it above our physical reach but not beyond our self-deluding reveries. Here, in the exhibition ballroom dancers, were we ourselves as we would have liked to imagine we appeared to others.

Danger is also a major element in dance diversion. The acrobatic dancer and even the classical ballerina exploit peril. The ballerina usually combines danger with beauty of action, musical stimulus and dramatic purposes so that her dancing becomes more than merely diverting; but daring, whether it is used by the artist or the entertainer, is a valid and highly effective dance commodity. Whether seeds of barbarism still exist in us or not may be debatable, but we all like to watch actions which could, with one misstep, lead to disaster. Usually the dancer challenges the law of gravity, and if he loses he can pay with anything from his pride to his neck. In leaps, in precarious balances, in flips in air, in dizzying turns, in split-timed tricks with partners, the dancer dares gravity to do its worst, and as we watch, leaning forward in our seats, we share in the excitement of peril without wagering our own safety.

The danger of dancing provides an exaggerated example of that aesthetic which is the special province of dance. If a dancer appears to be on the verge of falling or slipping, we automatically try to recover for him, although we are in no danger at all. Such response to the movement of others is instinctive. With dance, it merely requires cultivation.

Looking at the action of dance is simple, but to really see the action of dance one must see with his body and not with his eyes alone. Just as the color of a painting remains photographed in the mind when the eyes are closed, or the echo of a tune stays in the ear memory long after the actual sounds have ceased, so should the muscles of the onlooker respond to and remember the movements of dance.

If we hold ourselves tense as the acrobat does his somersault, we can also, with a bit of muscle tuning, actually feel the invitation implicit in an extended hand, the exhilaration of a leg swept high or the anguish mirrored in a dancing body bent double and harshly contracted. If the dancer's body is erect, do we see merely an upright figure or do we recognize—because we have felt it ourselves—pride or assurance or authority? And if the dancer's muscles are contracted, bending his body low, do we see simply a bent pattern or do we remember the spasms which afflicted us, the broken arch of the spine when we ourselves experienced loss or pain or defeat?

With this aesthetic, called kinesthetics by the dancer, one is equipped to find more than physical diversion or entertaining prowess in dancing. It is possible, then, to journey with the dancer along the paths of adventure created by the choreographer. Not everything will be pretty, for dance is no more limited to prettiness than is painting or literature or drama, but the journey will be stirring, perhaps even illuminating.

Where, one may ask, will such journeys lead us? In such classical ballets as *The Sleeping Beauty* or *Swan Lake* the trip is to fairyland, but in certain contemporary dramatic ballets the travels go deep into the human heart, there to explore very real passions and temptations. In other instances there will be no narrative, no plot, but we will see dancing bodies reflect the rhythms and the phrases of great music, transforming sound into substance or reacting to the urgings, both physical and emotional, of the score.

In America's modern dance, born free of the traditions of the classical ballet, we may find anything from satire to celebration, a satire such as Martha Graham's *Every Soul Is a Circus,* in which an empty-headed, selfish woman fancies herself queen of all she surveys, or a celebration, such as Doris Humphrey's *Day on Earth,* in which the dignity of man, his labors, his play and his love, his sweet relationship, sometimes joyous and again sorrowful, with wife and child, all speak through the movements of dance.

On other occasions, dance may speak for an entire race and not merely for the individual. In the flashing dances of Spain, in the profound religious dance dramas of India, in the poetic patterns of Japanese theater or in the ceremonies of Bali, no single choreographer is speaking his views, but rather is a nation presenting its heritage to the viewer. For the ethnic dance arts are the work of thousands of creative spirits over hundreds and thousands of years, and in these dances one sees, in capsule form, the history, the customs, the faiths, the ideals, even the temperament of a given nation. Because of their exotic surfaces, such ethnic dances are wholly diverting, but beneath their strange glitter lie treasure houses of learning.

This theater dance, with its vast range of material and with its ability to amuse or challenge or disturb, lives and thrives not only as an independent art but also as a contributor to other forms of theatrical fare. It serves opera, musical comedy, movies, television and even drama, lending its physical skills, its silent eloquence to any theatrical project which can use them.

Who, in America, looks at dancing today? Practically everybody, for dance is now almost inescapable. Until shortly after the turn of the century audiences for dance were limited. Although George Washington enjoyed the ballet and although ballet itself had its vogues and its fadings since colonial times, audiences were generally urban, cosmopolitan, sophisticated. Somehow, ballet did not seem to belong to the public at large.

Slowly but sturdily, theatrical dancing in America found its roots and commenced to grow, to attract the attention of the majority. Anna Pavlova, the great Russian ballerina, had done her pioneering for the ballet just as Ruth St. Denis, Ted Shawn and their Denishawn Dancers pioneered for free dance forms and ethnic dance importations.

In 1933 there was but one major ballet company in America, touring briefly and limiting itself to a short New York season. Twenty years later there were several ballet companies enjoying successful travels on the road and playing to enormous audiences for long engagements in New York and other cities. Other forms of dance, native and foreign, experienced a similar response from the public.

Put into cold figures, the American public's limited interest in dance productions caused the noted impresario, S. Hurok, to lose something close to $100,000 on his dance

9

attractions in 1933. Twenty years later a much more interested public enabled the same impresario to gross over four
million dollars on his dance presentations alone. Something
had happened in twenty years. A vast audience for dancing
had come into being. By 1971 not only were there ballet,
modern dance and ethnic troupes performing extended engagements—some ballet companies were performing as much
as forty-five or fifty weeks out of the year—but also ballet
groups of great merit had sprung up across the entire United
States.

Movies helped carry theater dance forms to a great many
who would not otherwise have known of their existence. The
introduction of ballets and serious dance creations into
musical comedies not only enriched the lyric theater itself
but also let audiences know that ballet and concert dance
forms were not difficult to understand, not beyond their
range of enjoyment.

And television, of course, carried all kinds of dancing into
the home. Although the new medium often contented itself
with diverting dances, with hoofing routines and dance versions of popular songs, it also introduced great ballet artists
to a new and broader public and it even dared to experiment
with highly intellectual, emotionally adult dance creations.
Dancing, by way of television, had made friends with onetime strangers and worked its magic so thoroughly that little
girls wanted to become ballerinas while their older brothers
and sisters and their parents found it fun to go to their
community theaters and auditoriums to see their ballet favorites in the flesh and to witness the spectacle of dance as it
could be seen only on the stage.

Dance Landscape

To the average American, dance has not yet become the necessity it was (and is) to the American Indian, for the average American is mainly an onlooker and not, except in the social sense, a participant. Yet at last, after centuries of ups and downs, ins and outs, dance has become established in the American theater, no longer a suspect, if attractive, stranger but a citizen.

There are many who can take the art of dancing or leave it alone, but there are, these days, few who avoid it because "I wouldn't understand it." For dancing figures are now a part of our landscape. And these figures are not all alike. They are a line of pretty girls kicking together in splendid unison, but they are also a company of stalwart youths projecting through movement the powers, the beauties, the duties of democracy. One figure is a ballerina perched exquisitely upon the tiny point of her toe slipper and another is a woman revealing through dance those secret fears which must be met and conquered if a soul is not to be destroyed.

They are also figures of joy leaping toward the heavens and figures of tenderness encircling the miracle of a child. They spin in terror or in ecstasy, they step with prideful tread or defeated stumble, they gesture sensually or prayerfully, they run with carefree exuberance or speed into the core of conflict. They are endless, these figures who populate the American dance scene. But their journey was hard and often lonely, for they started out before the dawn of recorded history.

2

Dances of Antiquity—
The Coming of the Ballet

The art of dancing, to many Americans, seems like a novelty, something of recent invention. Because it is comparatively new to the American scene (on a large scale, at least), even distinguished writers of art appreciation, of history, of philosophy tend to ignore it. Yet without dance it is highly unlikely that such writers would have been able to discuss music or drama or poetry . . . for dancing came first.

In hot aesthetic discussions—and scholars can argue as hotly as politicians—the dancer's view that his is the oldest of the arts is invariably met with a snorting "Prove it!" The age of dance is not especially important if the disputants are working on the childish level of possessiveness in which the statement "My art is older than yours" is little better than "My dolly is prettier than yours" or "My daddy can beat your daddy." What is important to establish in the mind of the newcomer to dance is that dance is a primary art, that it is "first" not merely chronologically but "first" in instinct.

Movement is the prime manifestation of life itself and movement is the prime element of dance. Dancing, indeed, is older than man himself. Animals and birds have their dances of courtship, patterns of action which are easily recognizable as formal dances. There is neither wishful thinking nor self-delusion on the part of dancers here, for naturalists have reported and filmed such dances on numerous occasions.

In a very real sense, the movement, the rhythm and the order of the universe constitute an enormous ballet, and more than one ancient race thought of the stars as dancing in the hcavcns or themselves composed astral dances which mirrored, at least to their satisfaction, the movements of sun, moon, planets, stars. But even before civilized man related his dances to cosmic forces, early man, by instinct, danced.

He had many reasons for dancing. He danced to release energy, he danced to demonstrate his prowess, he danced to celebrate a kill, he danced because his sex desires led him into dances of courtship, he danced to communicate an event or an idea or a feeling and he danced in order to make a magic strong enough to control or propitiate those mysterious and seemingly ungovernable forces of nature which surrounded him.

At first, in his dances of magic, he imitated nature, thereby identifying himself with the powers he hoped to control. Perhaps his stamping feet would echo to the heavens, bringing responsive thunder and life-giving rain. Later, he came to believe that the wind or a stream or a tree were not in themselves gods but that they were inhabited by unseen deities, and he built for himself, over centuries and millennia, symbol dances in which direct imitation gave way to ceremonies presumably pleasing to the deity adored.

And lastly, man found that deity could live within himself, and thus his body became a temple and place which could be purified through dance so that it would become a fitting home for God.

But what of the art of dance? Here, in the primitive dances of early man, the activity of dance could be found, but it was not yet an art form and it did not become one until a priesthood evolved certain magical or religious dances which were to be observed by the worshiper rather than performed by him. The priests, thereby, became performers, specialists in dance. In sacred settings the theater of dance was born.

Little of the heritage of the sacred dance has survived in America's churches and temples. Occasionally, however, religious dances are performed in houses of worship, at ecclesiastical gatherings and even on television, but for the most part the sacred dance and its derivatives have found their American home in the theater.

The religious dance rituals of the ancient Egyptians; the ceremonial, choric, athletic and military dances of the Greeks; and the ecstatic, prophetic dances of the Israelites have been crushed, in a literal sense, by the passage of time. There have been revivals, of course, of Greek games and the classic chorus of the Greek drama, and it is quite true that contemporary dervishes in the Middle East have a ballet similar in purpose and perhaps in form to the astral dances of the Egyptians of antiquity. Mainly, however, what have come down to us are proven principles of dance usage.

Dances of Antiquity—The Ballet

The purpose of David dancing before the Ark "with all his might" was not much different from that of the American Shakers of the eighteenth and nineteenth centuries who shed sins through the shaking of their bodies in services closely allied to dancing. And the self-induced ecstasy of the sacred dance of David and of the prophets could be shorn of its sacerdotal meanings and serve the secular dance excitingly. Except in highness of purpose, there is physically little difference between the whirling dervish and the ballerina spinning on the point of her toe slipper to storms of applause.

The Western dance theater has taken for its heritage the substances, the principles, the overtness, the physicality of primitive dances and ancient ceremonies rather than their forms. The East has pursued a different course, for the classical dance of India was nurtured thousands of years ago and retains to this day its ancient gesture language and its overwhelmingly religious cast. Indeed, almost every ballet in the vast repertory of Indian dance treats with legends of the gods, with man's relationship to deity, with religious allegories. And although the dance of India (comprising the four great schools of Bharat Natyam, Kathakali, Kathak and Manipuri) and the dance cultures it helped to mother (those of Siam, Cambodia, Indonesia, etc.), as well as the highly developed dance art of Japan, have their moments of violence and freely released ecstasy, they all tend toward serenity, toward richly detailed but nonflamboyant action.

America's dance art of today has drawn nourishment from the olden heritages of both East and West and from the ever-invigorating and recurring primitive sources. Our acceptance and application of Oriental dance materials have been comparatively recent while the dance heritage of our Biblical ancestors and their contemporaries has been channeled to us through the classical theater of Greece, through Roman pantomimes, the Italian *commedia dell' arte,* the noble banquet fetes and entertainments of the Renaissance and through the classical ballet which had its beginnings at about the time Columbus set out on his voyages of discovery.

That the West, quite unlike the East, filtered the sacred dance right out of its heritage was, of course, the doing of the Christian church. Religious leaders of the early church, believing that dancing was too closely associated with pagan rites, perhaps wistfully remembered by some, discouraged dancing and, fearing secular influences in the services, banned it from the church itself. Both dance and drama, which had long known a home in the temple and in certain churches, found themselves pushed beyond the sacred portals and there was nothing for them to do but go their secular ways.

There were exceptions. Sacred dancing survived, through special permission, in certain cathedrals for certain ceremonies and in some Eastern branches of the Christian church, and it is still to be found by the vigilant searcher. But the general ban did its work thoroughly, and a potential liturgy of sacred dance, comparable to the vast library of sacred music which is our heritage, did not materialize.

Bans or no bans, people danced, and if they could not dance in their churches, they danced elsewhere, in their homes, in the fields, in the streets. Pre-Christian religious dances survived as folk dances (the Maypole dance, once a fertility ceremony, is an example), and the combination of physical, emotional and spiritual energies which once had found outlet in ecstatic services and rites occasionally found itself perverted by superstition and emerged in such frightening guises as the dance mania which swept Europe in the Middle Ages.

But it was dance as a secular activity, propagated by the folk and polished by the nobility, which led to that great classic art of the Western world which we now call "ballet."

Ballet had its inception in the late fifteenth-century ducal courts of Italy. It wasn't ballet as we know it today, for the participants were amateurs, the toe slipper was absent from the scene and that vast vocabulary of steps and movements through which ballet now speaks had not yet been invented. But the ingredients of ballet—dancing, music, décor, storytelling—were there. Eating, however, was the main ingredient, for these spectacles were presented in conjunction with banquets, with celebrations of the most lavish sort.

At such fetes, figures representing the gods and heroes of antiquity would appear in processionals or in pantomimes; poetry would be declaimed and songs sung; gorgeous costumes, elaborate settings, the elements of spectacle would be present; and dining by a resplendent assembly of distinguished guests would be enjoyed. For dancing, we would have witnessed the court dances of the day, pantomimic motions and, perhaps, some actions which might have been viewed as eccentric or character dancing.

The revival of drama during the Italian Renaissance also brought with it opportunities for dancers to perform between the acts or scenes of the plays, and from these modest but popular beginnings and from the banquet fetes themselves, the art of ballet commenced to take form. A century of fetes, masques, processionals, pantomimes and incidental dances at last culminated in what is now referred to as the first ballet, *Le Ballet Comique de la Reine,* produced in Paris in 1581 by the Italian-born Queen of France, Catherine de Médicis.

In this history-making production, all the elements of spectacle had been united into a dramatic whole choreographed by Balthazar de Beaujoyeulx (also Italian by birth), the first major creator in the art of ballet. This new form of entertainment, which had taken five or six hours to unfold and which had cost Catherine millions of francs, also earned for her the envious admiration of other European courts. And because of its success, the *Ballet Comique* led to the fostering of dance and choreography in masques, interludes and in that form of presentation which resembled, more closely than anything else, a combination of opera and ballet.

With the coming of Louis XIV to the throne of France, ballet entered its first period of swift and brilliant growth. In 1661 the King established the Royal Academy of Dancing, and twenty years later the first professional female dance star in the history of ballet, Mlle. Lafontaine, made her debut. The King himself and the courtiers continued to appear in ballets, but with the development of professional dancers under the direction of Pierre Beauchamp (the first ballet master at the Royal Academy) and of Lully, the great composer, ballet in France attained a peak of eminence which was to go unrivaled, if not unchallenged, by other nations for years to come.

During the eighteenth century the Paris Opéra nurtured the special talents of Marie Camargo, who freed the female dancer of her floor-length skirts, invented new steps and stressed dancing *en air* rather than *à terre;* Marie Sallé, who also rid the feminine form of many encumbrances of costume, gave special accent to the drama of dance and became one of the first female choreographers; Gaetan and Auguste Vestris (father and son), unrivaled exponents of male dancing; and Jean Georges Noverre, the great choreographer, innovator, dance reformer and author of *Letters on Dancing and Ballets.*

The same century also witnessed the growth of ballet activity in London, Milan, Copenhagen, Vienna, St. Petersburg and other great cities, and performers and teachers, ballet masters and choreographers from France and from Italy led the swift expansion of ballet across the continent. Native sons and daughters of many lands also served the art, but the Paris Opéra remained the capital of the ballet world and the French and the Italians held the major posts of command.

With the nineteenth century came the demise of classical themes in ballet, the end to tales of the gods and goddesses of old. Romance was in the air, and folk legends of Europe, fantasies, lyricisms captured the ballet. The female dancer—one of the first was the great Marie Taglioni—rose onto the very point of her toes, thus escaping reality for an excursion into the new Romantic Age and, incidentally, causing a whole new technique of balletic action to be born.

Taglioni, light and spiritual, and her greatest rival, Fanny

Elssler, earthy and fiery, were the opposing yet complementary symbols of this Romantic Age, and sharing it with them in the middle years of the century were such ballerinas as Carlotta Grisi, star of the first *Giselle* (1841), Fanny Cerito and Lucile Grahn. Here were the real stars of the theater, commanding high salaries, respect and popular adoration.

America, since the time of the American Revolution, had also been enjoying ballet, both native and imported, and had even sent one dancer, Augusta Maywood, abroad to become the first American ballerina to be placed by the European public on a par with European ballerinas. But America's period of ballet power was yet to come.

Indeed, in the late nineteenth century Paris was to lose much of its leadership as national ballets grew up and matured in other lands and as the center of ballet creativity shifted, in a great degree, toward Russia.

Under the direction of Marius Petipa, with Lev Ivanov as his assistant, the Russian Imperial Ballet brought new splendor to the art. From Italy came Virginia Zucchi and Pierina Legnani to introduce great acting skills and undreamed-of virtuosities to the Russian ballet public and to inspire Petipa with their remarkable abilities while challenging Russian-born dancers to equal them. Such enduring classics as *The Sleeping Beauty, Swan Lake* and *The Nutcracker* were born, in addition to a host of other ballets which served their shorter lifetimes honorably and imaginatively.

With these ballets and with the coming of such great Russian performers as Mathilde Kchessinska, Olga Preobrajenska, Anna Pavlova, Tamara Karsavina, Vaslav Nijinsky and Michel Fokine, whose dancing career was somewhat obscured by his genius as a choreographer, it was small wonder that in the minds of many the word "ballet" and the descriptive term "Russian" were undivorceable.

But perhaps Russian ballet would not have become as lastingly influential as it did if it had not been for the travelings of Pavlova and the vision of a man who was neither a dancer nor a choreographer. This man was Serge Diaghilev, who took a company of Russian dancers to Paris in 1909 and electrified the world. He not only fostered the choreographic reforms of Fokine, who himself had revitalized the ballet which had been carrying on a Petipa formula, but he also united the talents of great composers, painters, librettists, choreographers and dancers to build the most exciting theater of dance that the world had yet seen.

From 1909 to 1929 the stages of Europe and, occasionally, America came alive with the vivid colors and fresh movements of Fokine's *Firebird, Petrouchka, Prince Igor* and the loveliness of *Le Spectre de la Rose* and *Les Sylphides.* Other Fokine ballets and vital creations by Nijinsky, Nijinska, the youthful Leonide Massine and George Balanchine made the repertory of Diaghilev's Ballets Russes unequaled in the world of dance.

With Diaghilev's death in 1929, the whole structure of Western ballet seemed to fall apart. Fokine, Massine, Balanchine and the dancers went their separate ways.

By 1931 and 1932 new ballet drives were launched. Ninette de Valois opened a school and formed a ballet unit which were to grow into the world-famous Sadler's Wells

Ballet, and Colonel W. de Basil and René Blum, gathering together some of the artists of the Diaghilev company, founded the Ballet Russe de Monte Carlo.

In 1933 the Ballet Russe de Monte Carlo arrived for its first performances in America, and with its coming a new era of ballet began, an era which would see the firm establishment of ballet in America, the growth of American ballet itself and an opportunity for America to become the center of activity for one of the greatest international art forms that the world has yet produced.

3

Dance in Colonial America

*American colonists—English, French, Spanish—found, re-*ported on and, in certain instances, recorded through draw-ings and descriptive texts the dances of the Indians living in their areas of exploration and conquest. To some, the dances of the aboriginal inhabitants seemed savage, licentious, pagan, while to the more sensitive reporters, the rich cere-mony, the complex patterns and the intricate movements devised by certain tribes were immediately apparent.

But the colonists did not merely record, admire, reject or ignore the dances they found in the New World; they also brought their own dances with them. If, at first, they had little time for dancing, ultimately fetes and divertissements which included dancing were arranged by the wealthy in the growing cities and by governing officials. Meanwhile, the poorer folk availed themselves of their few moments of re-laxation to join with their neighbors in dancing and, when possible, to send their daughters to dancing school to learn deportment and grace. For even in the rough New World refinement was not forgotten.

All was not, however, smooth sailing for dance and dancers. The Puritans, who were not nearly as antidance as some of their historians have made out, did not, on the other hand, go out of their way to establish an American dance culture. They made it quite clear that they respected and admired the Bible's approval of dancing, and they wistfully suggested that if the colonists would engage in the kind of dancing described in the Bible there would be no trouble at all. What they did object to was mixed dancing for men and women, dances which conceivably might generate an attitude of licentiousness and dances done by professional performers.

Actually, the professional performer, be he actor, singer, acrobat or dancer, was regarded with suspicion by the Northern colonists, and the bans which descended occasionally on the theater and dancing academies in Boston, New York or Philadelphia in colonial and post-Revolutionary times were quite probably caused by the fairly universal belief that theatrical folk, who did not earn their livings in homely trades or accepted business enterprises, tended to be immoral. This notion that there is something racy, something not-quite-nice about the theatrical performer, and the dancer in particular, has survived down to our own times.

The Puritans, then, did not ban dancing. They banned certain kinds of dancing, and these distinctions they made quite clear in a famous treatise called "An Arrow Against Profane and Promiscuous Dancing . . ." prepared by a group of Boston ministers.

In the early decades of the eighteenth century, tentative

excursions into dramatic presentations by amateur and semi-professional groups often included dancing. Jigs and horn-pipes were popular, dances performed on tightropes were particularly admired, and one may be certain that high jinks of a rhythmic nature were incorporated into those panto-mimes peopled by Harlequin, Scaramouche and other figures descending from the tradition of the old European *commedia dell' arte.*

By the middle of the century professional troupes such as the one headed by Lewis Hallam arrived in America to treat the American colonists to plays, the ever-popular harlequin-ades, spectacles and incidental dances, and in 1768 the first American dancer of note, John Durang, was born.

Durang, presumably self-taught, made his debut in Phila-delphia in 1784, and although he danced many roles and tried his hand at choreography, he earned his greatest fame with his *Hornpipe.* During his long and successful career this *Hornpipe* turned up again and again, and such was its popu-lar appeal that the music for "Durang's Hornpipe" was pub-lished and a detailed description, step by step, of his dance patterns was recorded by his son, Charles, who also became a dancer.

Whether Durang was unusually gifted or whether his nationality provided him with unusual opportunities would be hard to say. Certainly, the fact he was the only American-born member of Hallam's troupe, which returned to America following the Revolution, was of inestimable help to him, for the newly independent nation and its citizens were not overly friendly toward English artists.

But it is likely that Durang was a dancer of natural gifts

and that through association with trained artists from the continent he learned his craft well and disciplined his inborn talents for use in the professional theater.

Through the years with Hallam, with the French Alexander Placide and his company and with other groups, Durang performed such classical dances as the minuet and *allemande,* enacted the role of Harlequin in an endless array of harlequinades, danced with Gardie (a popular ballerina of the day), performed variations of his *Hornpipe* (on tightropes and even on eggs!) and was a participant in productions given in New York which George Washington attended.

During the period right after the American Revolution, all theatrical companies stressed patriotic pageants. *The Patriot, or Liberty Asserted; The Independence of America, or the Ever Memorable 4th of July, 1776;* and *The American Heroine* were but a few of the patriotic displays presented for the public's pleasure and, one may assume, with the fond hope that such offerings would help dispel that air of suspicion which continued to surround theatrical performers.

Although patriotic spectacles were of major concern, other productions were mounted: romances, farces, pastoral ballets closely allied to the traditions of the Paris Opéra and, of course, scenes which employed the talents of specialty dancers, acrobats and the enduring tightrope dancers.

Far from the theater but equally theatrical in potential were the danced ceremonies of the Shakers, a religious sect which centered its communities in the eastern part of New York State, in New England and, after the turn of the nineteenth century, in the Middle West. But it was during the

American Revolution that the Shakers first established themselves firmly in the New World.

Their faith, which they had brought with them from England, barred them from marriage and all sexual relationships and focused their attention upon the creation of a sinless society in the New World. Like ancient sects which preceded them, they believed that angels danced in heaven and, like the Biblical prophets of old, found communion with divinity in ecstatic but ordered dancing. Through dancing, then, sin could be shaken from their bodies.

In their earliest dances (in the nineteenth century many elaborations would be introduced) the worshipers moved in square-dance form, with shuffling steps which carried them advancing and retreating. Men and women moved in separate groups, holding their hands in front of them, chanting and, if one can judge from the old prints of Shaker services and from the memories of still living Shakers (whose rituals, of course, were slightly different from those of Revolutionary days), vibrating hands and bodies as they moved forward and back, turned and bent their bodies in supplication or lifted heads high in ecstasy.

At first glance, it seems strange that a religious society building its rituals upon dance action should spring up during the eighteenth century in a nation which could never quite decide whether to ban dancing or not and in which the Puritan tradition was strong. But one must remember that the Shakers were not show folk, that mixed dancing was not a part of their service and that they were in perfect accord with Puritan sensibilities with respect to the validity of a way of dancing derived from spiritual, Biblical sources.

And although the Shakers contributed nothing to the theater dance of their era, they kept alive in the New World a concept of religious dance deriving from Christian, and not pagan, sources, and in later generations their lively yet consecrated efforts would stimulate dance creativeness in choreographers of the twentieth century's dance theater.

But if the dancing of the Shakers was isolated from the rest of American behavior patterns and if theatrical dancing wove its difficult course between popular appreciation and governmental disapproval, social dancing among the aristocrats of the New World commenced to thrive. Washington himself danced and members of his government were quick to recognize the value of social-dance instruction for their children. The new nation needed moments of relaxation, and it needed to partake of an elegance flaunted, on all possible occasions, by the Old World. These it found in the social dances of the day, in the formalities of rhythmic and ordered movement.

The ordinary folk also danced measures brought by their pioneering forebears from the mother nations beyond the seas, learned the steps of new dances imported from abroad, and as the young republic passed from the eighteenth to the nineteenth century, it found time to originate the barn dance, the Virginia reel, the clog, the Paul Jones and the cakewalk as the decades passed and styles changed.

Though some ministers of the church may have frowned upon theatrical dancing, many of them danced themselves, and though the professional performers frequently had to disguise their presentations as "lectures," in order to skirt rulings against the theater, they managed to keep the theater, and theatrical dancing, alive. In the new United States of America the spirit of dance was present in some form for almost every walk of life. It was not essential to living, as it was to the Indians, but it was, obviously, desirable.

4

American Scene: The 1800's

Nineteenth-century Americans, suffering from a rather de-
fiant inferiority complex, were faced with the constant re-
minder that culture had to be imported from abroad, and
although they were devoted to the American-born John
Durang, who started his career in the late eighteenth century,
they were intensely eager to see and to play host to European
dancers. There were French invasions and Italian invasions,
but America in this century managed to produce several
dancers of uncommon distinction. Among them were Mary
Ann Lee, Julia Turnbull, George Washington Smith (certainly the nation's first genuine premier danseur) and Augusta Maywood. With Maywood, America turned the tables
on Europe, for the highly talented girl reversed the invasion
in triumphant fashion.

As La Petite Augusta, Maywood made a successful debut in
her native Philadelphia in 1837, and two years later, following a series of highly praised performances in her homeland,

she became, at the age of fifteen, the first American to be engaged as première danseuse at the hallowed Paris Opéra. She captivated both public and critics in Paris and, with this solid and enviable approval behind her, went on to continuing successes in European cities for more than twenty years. Indeed, she was held in such esteem that the title of *prima ballerina e prima mima assoluta,* the highest recognition of dance artistry to be given in Italy, was hers, a post shared by only one other dancer of that period, Fanny Elssler.

Another Philadelphia girl, Mary Ann Lee, who had made her debut as a child on the same program with her contemporary, Maywood, centered her brief but brilliant career in her own land. Although she acted, sang and danced specialty numbers, her fame rests upon her dancing as an exponent of the classical ballet.

Following her New York debut in 1839, Mary Ann Lee appeared in a series of ballets which ranged from American versions of European ballet favorites to original creations. She learned and performed dances associated with Elssler, who began a sensational two-year tour of America in 1840, and she also appeared in a burlesque of *La Bayadère or the Maid of Cashmere,* one of her favorite works, which enjoyed the pun-laden title of "Buy It Dear, 'Tis Made of Cashmere."

In 1844 she left her loyal American public for a year abroad and devoted it to intensive study at the school of the Paris Opéra. When she returned home, she was equipped to present in authentic form several of the major ballet creations popular in Europe at the time. Among them was *Giselle,* which she introduced to America, and, since she had studied with the choreographer, Jean Coralli, and pre-

31

sumably had seen Carlotta Grisi, the originator of the title part, perform it in Paris, one may be certain that she gave her followers an accurate recreation of a ballet destined for immortality.

If Mary Ann Lee had an American rival on the American dance scene, it was Julia Turnbull, an accomplished dancer and mime who appeared on bills with her rival, with George Washington Smith and with other dancers of note. Because her career outlasted that of the frail Mary Ann Lee, she was able to enjoy a period of unchallenged rule as the most popular American ballerina.

George Washington Smith, another Philadelphian, may quite properly be treated as the first premier danseur produced by America, for although he performed pantomimic, comedy and character parts, he also excelled in those romantic ballets which called for the presence of a premier danseur noble.

His career began at about the same time as those of Maywood and Lee, but it was to last until the close of the century. During this long period, he developed from a hornpipe and clog dancer to an artist good enough to appear with Elssler; to dance the principal male roles in *Giselle, La Fille du Danube* and other popular works of the age; to choreograph, direct and produce and, long after the Civil War, to turn his talents to teaching.

Existing photographs of George Washington Smith may not mirror our own ideas of what a premier danseur should look like, for the bushy mustache seems to overbalance all other physical attributes. But in the stiff poses of a dancer photographed when he was past middle age, we can discern legs which are slim and strong, a slender but manly build and an air of elegance and authority. Photographs, however, are not needed to prove the importance of G. W. Smith, dancer, for his name is a recurring theme in the annals of nineteenth-century ballet in America.

The American artists, then, held their own against the invaders with respect to artistry, but their numbers were small in comparison with the many stars who journeyed to these shores to be warmly welcomed by the American theatergoing public. And no one received a warmer welcome than Fanny Elssler. Wine was drunk from her slipper, the Congress of the United States adjourned that its members might not miss her performance and the dollars poured in at the box office. A brief visit turned into a two-year stay, an extended triumphal.

There were, of course, other dancers from Europe—French, Italian, English, even Russian—who held the ballet at a peak of importance during much of the 1800's. There were, for example, Giovanna Ciocca, a rival to Turnbull; the Ronzi-Vestris family, related to one of ballet's greatest dynasties; Mme. Augusta (not Maywood) ; the Ronzani troupe; Lola Montez, not the most brilliant of dancers but a vivid personality; and still more.

The biggest ballet splurge of the nineteenth century occurred in 1866, when the extravaganza *The Black Crook* opened in New York with a cast headed by Marie Bonfanti, Rita Sangalli and Betty Regal. This six-hour showpiece ran for two years in New York with additions, deletions and changes occurring from time to time, but no matter how it was altered, the ballet sections constituted the hit of the program. Few, apparently, were very much impressed with the drama of *The Black Crook*, but Bonfanti, her colleagues and the "fifty auxilliary ladies" thoroughly aroused the interest of New Yorkers.

So successful was *The Black Crook* that within a week of its closing the producers came up with a quick imitation, *The White Fawn*, and once again the ballet, with Bonfanti as the star, received the greatest praise.

Not all was ballet in nineteenth-century America. The minstrel show introduced the blackface singers and dancers and, belatedly, black performers themselves. There were Daddy Rice (a white man), famous as Jim Crow with his jigs and shuffles; Juba (a Negro), who took his name from an African-derived dance step and was hailed as one of the greatest dancers of the 1840's, and there were such famed troupes as the Christy Minstrels.

Always, though, the Negro minstrel and the white minstrel in blackface were clowns. The physical agility, the fabulous rhythms, the great performing gifts of the Negro were utilized but channeled into set molds. He was a comic, he was an eccentric, he could be an exotic, he might be a virtuoso, but he was invariably a joyous soul on vacation from the happy life of the old plantation. Not until the twentieth century rolled around would the American Negro have an opportunity to be himself and to explore and exploit the vast range of his inherent artistry.

But the minstrel era, which crossed an entire century, brought the Negro with his dance and music onto the stage, and it brought endless delight to audiences not only in America but also in highly critical Europe. And from the black dancer, and the influences he brought to bear on his white associates with the clog dances, came one of the most popular of all theatrical dance forms, tap (see Chapter 12 on "The Black Dance") .

With the establishment of vaudeville in the late nineteenth century, variety—including variety in dance—became the rage. Ballet dancers, tap dancers, eccentric dancers, lovely chorus girls, skirt dancers and the like brought together in a potpourri the styles, if not always the stylishness, enjoying the popular approval of the moment.

Not all dancing, however, was housed in the theater. Recreational dance had its legion of followers as it had had from the time of George Washington. There were balls and barn dances to attend, new steps to learn and teachers to instruct the young in grace and deportment and their elders in the latest social-dancing trends.

Folk dances from the old countries were becoming absorbed, altered and, in many instances, given new names, names as American as "Hull's Victory," "Jefferson and Liberty," "Constitution Hornpipe," "Portland Fancy" and the like.

Holding strict to the highest standards of ballroom dance in the nineteenth century was Allen Dodworth, whose Dancing Academy offered a system of instruction which placed ballroom dancing on an educational plane designed to promote love of beauty, rhythm, harmony, correct social behavior and even spirituality in his charges.

Dodworth and his family (he was succeeded late in the century by his nephew, George) guided the course of the Academy for almost one hundred years, from 1835 to 1920.

35

In his classes and in his writings (including his book *Dancing*, published in 1885) he carefully analyzed correct and incorrect ways of dancing, defined body positions, explained techniques of movement and rhythmic response and taught an endless array of students the quadrille, the waltz, the polka, the lancers and newer dances as they came along.

With New York as their headquarters, the Dodworths pretty much dictated to society the proper methods of dancing, and until George Dodworth helped found the New York Society of Teachers of Dancing just before the start of World War I, the Dodworth Academy remained aloof from all teachers' organizations, standing firm on the proven principles established with such lasting success by Allen when the nineteenth century was still young.

Part II

The Rebellion

5

Isadora Duncan—Loie Fuller

With the twentieth century came the spirit of rebellion. In Russia the young Michel Fokine commenced those choreographic experiments which were to lead toward the revitalizing of ballet. In America, where there was no Fokine, ballet was stagnant. Individual artists triumphed over material constricted by tired formulas, but dancing, though still a popular element in the American theater, was pretty much limited to prettified or acrobatic ballet, to tap dancers, to happy hoofing.

At the turn of the century, there were two young Americans who dreamed greater things for dancing than were to be found in the dances they saw about them. Their names were Isadora Duncan and Ruth St. Denis. Rejecting the weary ballet and what they felt was its emotional and spiritual emptiness, they claimed for their art values equivalent to those in the sister arts of music or drama, painting or literature. They were not concerned with steps as such, for they believed that the body, though trained, should be free to move expressively, free to communicate the profoundest thoughts and feelings of man.

"The highest intelligence in the freest body" was Isadora's goal. As a child in San Francisco—she had been born there in 1878—she rebelled against ballet instruction, certain that ballet technique was unbeautiful and quite against the laws of nature. Indeed, nature was her favorite teacher, and again and again she pointed out in her writings that the seas provided her with her earliest dance inspiration, that she studied "the movements of flowers and the flight of bees and the charming graces of pigeons and other birds" and that "dance is the movements of the human body in harmony with the movements of the earth." And Isadora's closeness to nature was by no means a matter of self-delusion. Mary Fanton Roberts has written beautifully of Isadora and nature in such luminous phrases as "and the sea and the wind and the sky accepted her in a mysterious comradeship" and "always she seemed a part of the great fundamental splendor of nature."

Isadora's life—restive, flamboyant, unconventional, triumphant, tragic—was centered in Europe. As a girl, hounded by poverty, she had done some teaching in San Francisco and later in New York, performed in productions by Augustin Daly both in New York and on the road, danced to the music of Ethelbert Nevin in recitals given by the young composer and augmented her precarious livelihood with appearances in the salons of the wealthy. But America, she felt, did not appreciate her genius and so, with begged and borrowed money, she and her family left for Europe.

The Duncans—Isadora, her mother, her sister Elizabeth and her brother Raymond (her brother Augustin remained in America)—found England equally unresponsive. There were performances for society but little else, particularly in the way of money. Studies in France came next, but Isadora's first major contract was for Budapest and here, in 1903, she danced for a month with tremendous success. Isadora was on her way.

In the ensuing years, until her death in an automobile accident in 1927 (she was strangled instantly when a fringed scarf she was wearing caught in the wheel of an open car—the scene is brilliantly recorded in a late 1960's movie, *The Loves of Isadora,* starring Vanessa Redgrave), she traveled across Europe, giving performances in the great cities, establishing her schools of the new and free dance and returning, on several occasions, to America, where her genius was at last recognized.

On her first visit to Russia in 1905, her vision of a free dance certainly influenced the young Fokine, for although he never divorced himself from the heritage of ballet itself, his plans for reform and Isadora's messages of liberation had much in common.

And Isadora's concept of dance came at a time when the art needed it most. She defied ballet convention and danced to the music of the great masters; she turned to ancient Greece not as a copyist but for inspiration; and she discovered that dancing was not predicated upon the movements of legs and arms but that it grew from an inner urge to action.

It was in Paris that she determined that the soul had its home in the solar plexus. As romantic as this may sound, she had found through her own instinct, or stumbled upon, a principle of movement which was to become a key element in the modern dance of the future. In her spirited autobiography *My Life* she wrote: "I was seeking and finally discovered the central spring of all movement, the crater of motor power, the unity from which all diversities of movements are born, the mirror of vision for the creation of the dance—it was from this discovery that was born the theory on which I founded my school."*

In her own time her brilliant, often anguished, unorthodox life tended to obscure, in the minds of many, her history-making artistry. She bore children without benefit of wedlock, she later married a Russian poet and became a Soviet citizen, she let herself get fat, she sometimes drank too much, she reacted with lasting agony to the drowning of her two children and she met her death through strangulation.

But fat or slim, depressed or ecstatic, she lived through and for dance. And if she found her greatest happiness and success abroad, she never lost sight of her vision of America dancing. She saw "great strides, leaps and bounds, lifted forehead and farflung arms, dancing the language of our pioneers, the fortitude of our heroes, the justice, kindness, purity of our women and through it all the inspired love and tenderness of our mothers, that will be America dancing."

Although she found inspiration in the spiritual purposes of the ancient Greek dance and was stimulated by the music of European composers, she was an American dancer of the present. She was stirred by the poetry of Walt Whitman,

* New York, Boni & Liveright, 1927.

42

perhaps influenced by the teachings (which had drifted to America) of François Delsarte on meaningfulness of gesture and movement; her immediate dance heritage was the Irish jig her grandmother knew, the American Indian dances which her forebears had seen on the trek westward and the movements of nature which she observed as a child.

Isadora, with her genius for movement, pooled her heritage with her own dance discoveries, and these were plentiful. Sometimes one thinks of her as a dancer of instinct, but extracting statements of principle from her scattered writings and her remarks to others, one discovers that Isadora was herself a discoverer of enormous perspicacity. In an era when the ballet had established the principle of defying gravity as a technical standard of dance execution, Isadora noted that "all movement on earth is governed by the law of gravitation, by attraction and repulsion, resistance and yielding; it is that which makes the rhythms of dance."

She also resented imitation, and not merely for reasons of jealousy. "Others," she said, "began to imitate me, not understanding that it was necessary to go back to a beginning, to find something in themselves first." She went on to say that "the dances of no two persons should be alike" and "I shall not teach the children to imitate my movements—I shall help them develop those movements natural to them."

Isadora, however, was not foolish enough to base her dance on the willingness of the spirit alone. She worked with the extension of movements from the solar plexus, she experimented successfully with sequential action in which one movement flowed into another, she recognized and used the force of gravity, she believed that "the teaching of sculpture

43

and dance should go hand in hand" and she even remarked, noting that the body should be developed physically for dance use, that "gymnastics and dancing should go together."

There is also a false notion that Isadora and her dancing children were mainly concerned with happy, pretty motions. Isadora's sister-in-law, Margherita, has commented that as Isadora grew older and tragedy had touched her, ugliness, when necessary, as well as beauty entered her dancing. She herself said, "Don't be merely graceful. Nobody is interested in a lot of graceful young girls. Unless your dancing springs from an inner emotion and expresses an idea, it will be meaningless."

Isadora danced to the music of Gluck and Schubert, Beethoven and Wagner and others of the great composers. She danced alone to symphonies almost as if she were a chorus in herself and, with passionate dedication, she gave dramatic form to the "Marseillaise" and the "Marche Slav," creating two of her testaments to man's battle for freedom. She danced on the great stages of the world and she danced in the moonlight in ancient Greek temples. She was an inspiration to painters and sculptors and she was a mother not only to her own children but to the hundreds of students who studied with her in whatever land she set up her studio or her temple of dancing.

When she died, her sister Elizabeth and some of the members of her adopted dancing family continued to teach her way of dancing, and although schools of Duncan dance still function and dancers of Duncan style still perform, it is the spirit of the inimitable Isadora itself which continues to exert the greatest influence on dance in America. She spent but few of her mature years in her native land, and so it was left to Ruth St. Denis and Ted Shawn to establish firmly a concept of the liberated dance in this nation, but as the decades pass, Isadora's monumental achievements loom ever larger and the knowing dancer of today fully realizes that the pulse of her discoveries is echoed in his own motions.

Another American innovator who found European surroundings more congenial than the American stage was Loie Fuller, who won fame for the quantities of materials she manipulated in her dances and for her elaborate lighting effects.

She was born in Illinois in 1862 and entered show business when still a small child. She was not, at first, a dancer. As an actress, she specialized in playing little-boy roles for many years, but she not only took part in plays, she also performed with the circus, in vaudeville and, in effect, appeared willing to take on any kind of a job which would keep her busy in the theater.

When she was about thirty, with years of experience in stock behind her, she stumbled upon a way of dancing which was to cause her to abandon her acting career for a new and revolutionary form of dance presentation.

Rehearsing in a play, which turned out to be a flop, she experimented with an enormous skirt in an effort to achieve a certain visual effect in one of the scenes. Lifting the skirt so that she wouldn't trip on it, she moved it so that it appeared to be an extension of her body in space. At the performance itself, the actions of Loie in her billowing skirt delighted the audience, causing them to compare her with a butterfly and then a flower.

From this first skirt dance—for it was related to the skirt dances popular in variety shows—she evolved her famous *Serpentine* and thereby launched a series of dances in which different-colored lights illuminated the materials.

In 1892 she went to Paris and became the rage of that city. With her flowing silks and gauzes and multiple lights, she transformed herself into a flame, into a butterfly, into a flower, and her stage into a magical land of lights. Hundreds of consecutive performances followed, with artists of all kinds joining the great mass of the public in their adoration of Loie Fuller and her new way of dancing.

She, like Isadora, tended more and more to use the music of the masters for accompaniment and, although she was apparently self-taught, she was concerned with the freedom of the body to move. But lights were all-important to her. For her *Flame Dance,* she moved on a pane of glass through which the lights streamed; later she made use of phosphorescent salts on materials to give her costumes luminosity, and at one point, in her own laboratory, she blew a sizable portion of her hair off during an explosion caused by her own experimentations.

Her inventions with light—and she was an inventor as well as an artist—served her throughout her long career and, indeed, revolutionized the art of theatrical lighting.

"La Loïe," as she came to be known, enjoyed triumphs throughout Europe, and on her visits to America she demanded and received high fees, attracted huge audiences and gained wide publicity for her performing, her lights and her extremely quotable comments on everything from science and art to social behavior.

Her last stage appearance was in 1926 in London. Two years later she was dead, leaving behind her a theater in Paris which bore her name; a band of Loie Fuller Girls, who continued to perform long after she was dead; memories of a much-publicized and slightly mysterious friendship with Queen Marie of Rumania; and a concept of theatrical lighting which made lighting not merely the antithesis of darkness but, rather, a living thing. "La Loïe" was a dancer, but for her a dancer was a creature of light, and in this unique capacity she illumined the stages of the world.

6

Ruth St. Denis

She appears to be a statue of bronze, graven in an attitude of serene dignity. The incense weaves upward, casting fragile shadows upon the image of the goddess, the threads of smoke breaking apart at brief intervals and permitting the light to catch the glow and the flash of jewels. The priest and the worshipers bow in prayer, traverse the ritual of adoration, and, through the force of their faith, the goddess of bronze comes to life. At first only the eyelids move, then the bosom slowly rises as the breath of living pours in, spreading to the trunk and limbs. The body seems to shimmer with subcutaneous action, with visceral activity, and soon the inner movement extends to surface muscles and the goddess steps down from her dais.

Radha, the deity, has a message for the faithful. Her eyes reflect the glitter of the jewels with which she is adorned; she plays with a strand of pearls and watches hungrily as its movements capture ever-changing degrees of light and glow.

Next, she places tiny finger cymbals on her hands and dances to their rhythms, bending her head near them to hear them strike, leaning away to listen to their overtones. A garland of flowers is pressed close to her face or swings in an arc about her moving body as she catches the fleeting echoes of scent.

From a cup, she sips, and it must be a heady wine, for the movements become quicker and freer, touched with a slight suggestion of reeling. Then her fingertips caress her skin, exploring the smoothness of arms and shoulders, and, as she sinks to the floor, she brings her hand upward in a high wide circle, bending her body back so that hand and lips meet in an ecstatic, self-adoring kiss. Each of the senses and its sensual outlet have been revealed.

Then the goddess covers her lower limbs with a skirt of gold and gives herself up to a delirium of the senses. The arms shudder in ecstasy, the body writhes in self-delight. The goddess commences to turn; faster and faster she moves, the skirt billowing gold fire about her, the head and body bending slowly backward until the peak of muscular abandon is reached. The spinning ceases and the figure slips to the floor.

Slowly she rises, allows the skirt of gold, symbol of earthly glitter, to fall from her, and with regal body, the serenity of renunciation upon her face, returns to the dais and reassumes her deity. Through her dance Radha has told her followers of the evils, the selfishness of a life predicated upon the senses alone and the sublime peace which comes from a renunciation of the sensual existence.

For almost half of the twentieth century the ballet *Radha* remained one of the most significant dance works of our time, as enduring as its creator, Ruth St. Denis. In later years it was almost impossible to witness it in dispassionate fashion, for it had become mellowed with nostalgia, flavored with sentiment, ennobled by history. Further, the continued presence of St. Denis in the role of Radha constituted something of a heart-warming phenomenon.

Radha is, however, a distinguished and powerful work, choreographically imaginative and eloquent in its conveying of a spiritual message. Oriental though it may be, audiences of the 1930's and 1940's (when St. Denis was in her sixties) were able to judge it on its own merits as a work of art (once they had accustomed themselves to the miracle of St. Denis dancing) and to recognize and accept its religious theme. There is, then, nothing in *Radha* to shock anyone any more, for its costumes are no longer considered daring, its movement patterns have long since altered the course of dance history and its mature handling of an adult theme is not foreign to the dance of today.

But in 1906, when *Radha* was first presented, the reaction of press and public was antithetic to the homage accorded it in later decades. St. Denis, *Radha* and a whole new way of dance were suddenly revealed to a public totally unprepared for them. America was used to the skirt dancers, the hoofers and to a bit of ballet—not the avant-garde ballet which the Russians were to introduce some years later, but pretty ballet, stunt toe dancing. Certainly, dancing was never meant to be anything but pleasant and innocuous and, perhaps, lively, at least as far as the 1906 generation was concerned. It is no wonder that St. Denis stole the headlines and caused sensation, confusion and argument.

At the time of her initial New York performances, the

headlines screamed: NO RUDE MEN MAY GAZE UPON THESE
SENSUOUS DANCES. MEN MUST PAY A WEEK LATER. OF COURSE,
SHE'S NOT ALL DRESSED, BUT IT'S ALL RIGHT TO THOSE WHO ARE
ORIENTAL; and another: NOT A HINDOO, ONLY A JERSEY BUD-
DHIST. TOMORROW NIGHT SHE WILL CAPER AS NIMBLY AT THE
NEW YORK THEATER AS SHE HAS AT MRS. STUYVESANT FISH'S.
. . . HER COSTUME? AH, WELL, SHE WEARS A LITTLE JACKET,
AND A SKIRT OF GAUZE AND MAYBE AN ANKLET OR TWO. Beneath the headlines ran stories such as this one: ". . . her
feet and ankles are also bare. . . . She will be discovered as a
statue of the idol Radha, which lady by the way was the
favorite wife of Krishna, a gallant sort of person who went
about tooting on a conch and winning women's hearts without number." Another headline referring to her tersely
stated: FOUNDS NEW CULT.

Boston, as was to be expected, outdid New York in react-
ing. The headlines literally yelped: BOSTON GASPS AS RUTH ST.
DENIS DANCES . . . SOCIETY REVIEWS ORIENTAL GYRATIONS IN
FENWAY PLACE . . . DARKNESS HID BLUSHES . . . BARE-
FOOT MAIDEN GIVES SOCIETY FOLK A NEW THRILL. A reporter
noted:

"Cold Roast" Boston sat up and took notice for about an
hour yesterday in Fenway Court and rubbed its eyes at
the spectacle of a bare-legged maiden who put the Persian
dancers on the Midway in the shade. . . . 250 representative men and women paid $5 for "sweet charity's sake"
to see her gyrations and contortions, and then they
gasped. . . . Ruth St. Denis was born on a New Jersey
farm which is a long way from Bombay and Calcutta.
Nevertheless she has hit the taste for novelties, and there

you are! Her stunts are truly sensational from any point of view, and yet none of her dances are open to the charges of vulgarity.

Probably no one will ever really know what Ruth St. Denis thought of such responses to her work. It is likely that, at the time, they hurt her spirit, for she had worked hard and with dedication to create *Radha,* yet her irrepressible humor unquestionably saved her from brooding sorrow. She often recalled the early days of *Radha* when, as she came onto the stage for rehearsal, the electricians would say, "Come on, boys, let's get the goddess lit."

Nor could she blame an unprepared public and press for their surprised reaction to her personal revolution. There were no standards by which to judge her. She was, it is believed, the first American dancer to appear in a full-length dance performance; she was the first American to use the profound themes of the Orient for her dances as distinct from the hootchy-kootchy activities of the "Fatimas" of the day; she built her dances upon a personally evolved technique of movement; she costumed herself not in keeping with the fashion of the times but in accord with the demands of her dances.

In their self-embarrassment, the reporters tried to review her on the basis of comparisons with other performers while admitting to the novelty of her offerings. They compared her with the "Persian dancers on the Midway" and then contradicted themselves flatly by concluding "none of her dances are open to the charges of vulgarity."

These very contradictions, these near-vulgar reports are both amusing and valuable. Their very "lostness" of manner proves the originality of the St. Denis work and the opening of America's dance revolution. And the self-conscious, brash, half-serious manner of their explanations suggests that not even untutored minds could dismiss her, that greatness was sensed if not recognized. So if these yellowed headlines are amusing to us in the light of history, they are also, in a perverse way, the bewildered heralds, the baffled recorders of triumph.

If the critics and audiences were excited and confused by the innovations of Ruth St. Denis, the dancer herself was in a similar frame of mind. Not that *Radha* confounded her; to the contrary, she knew what it meant to her and what its message was designed to convey, but the perspective of history was not yet hers. A good deal of what she had achieved was achieved through sheer instinct plus, of course, a divine gift of movement.

Reminiscing in 1947 she said, "For the first twenty years more or less I had no intellectual credo. I wasn't worrying about serving humanity. On the contrary, I agree entirely with Cabell, who maintains that the artist just plain does what he wants to do and the world can go hang as far as he is concerned. Only in later stages does he get explanatory."

If the "Jersey Hindoo" had no intellectual credo, or only a partial one, when *Radha* was born, she certainly possessed an inarticulate emotional credo which could not be denied. In retrospect, she would muse upon the pre-*Radha* period as one which would include

> every impulse to dance in childhood. . . . During this period I can only say that I was no different in my elemental urge to move my body to rhythm from any other child

since the world began, except that I had it stronger. During the farm period and later in vaudeville, I naturally moved and skipped about to both interior and exterior stimuli. In a word, I just hopped and skipped and sometimes waved my arms and lifted my head for the sheer inner ecstasy of living.

Obviously, I didn't have any ideas, I only had the deep cosmic impulse to move freely and rhythmically, which I believe is an inborn impulse carried over on the physical plane from the mere joy of youthful exuberance, as animals gambol in the spring. And from lambs gamboling in the spring, let us move to Himalayan heights where, according to my understanding of Hindu philosophy, the Gods dance because Brahma himself is sheer bliss and so *all* young things coming straight from God are happy. They cry because they can't yet reveal their joy but they begin bouncing on mother's knee and from there they indicate all their life that they came from a realm of light and joy and rhythm.

Behind the story of one who "had it stronger" is the tale of a little New Jersey farm lass who grew up to become one of the dance geniuses of all time. The child of an inventor father and a physician mother, Ruth Dennis had little formal training to prepare her for a dance career, or any career, for that matter. She bounded about the New Jersey farm, dancing on the grass, reading *Camille* at the age of eight while perched in the crotch of a tree, plowing through Kant's *Critique of Pure Reason* when she was twelve, not understanding it but stirred by it. A third and major book, one that influenced her life for her ninety-one years, was Mary Baker Eddy's *Science and Health*.

Ruth St. Denis

Her first performance occurred when she was three. At a barn dance with her parents, she reacted to the rhythms of the music and, with a tambourine placed in her tiny hands by her father, started "beating out the time, with some uncertain footwork to accompany it, a line of conduct I have followed ever since," as she describes it in her autobiography, *Ruth St. Denis: An Unfinished Life.**

Later came lessons in the movement technique of François Delsarte, ballroom dancing and something which probably passed for "aesthetic" dance. Somewhere along the line, she was able to work out some dance stunts, the kicks, the splits and the cartwheels of the skirt dancers of the day, and because of her Delsarte training and her native limberness, she was able to touch these tricks with a personal manner. The front kick was not so much a kick as a slow extension of the leg up to the head; the back kick was actually a kick to the back of the head and the split was done as a graceful sinking rather than as a jerking crash. There were also a few ballet lessons from Mme. Bonfanti, who had starred in *The Black Crook* in 1866, but St. Denis avers that she learned only three of the possible five classical positions of the feet and was tossed out of class.

The nearest Ruthie Dennis ever came to finishing-school training was a brief session at Dwight Moody's Seminary. This stint she finished with great dispatch and included Mr. Moody in the process. Irate when he learned of her interest in the theater and of her mother's active encouragement of such a life of sin, the reverend gentleman firmly lectured the

* New York, Harper & Brothers, 1939.

young lady only to be informed that he was a narrow-minded old bigot. On such an exit line, she left not only the office of Mr. Moody but also his school and returned to her family and to the theater.

With such a checkered background, a background of privately explored Eddy, Kant and Dumas, of local schooling and a Moody interlude, of sketchy studies in Delsarte, aesthetic dance and ballet, of constant encouragement at home, Ruth Dennis was ready to become a dancer and, ultimately, a great one. More important than any aspect of study, however, was the character of the girl herself. Here lay the boundless energy, the avid curiosity, the passion for beauty and the God-given genius which would make her succeed.

The early years of her professional life were as checkered as her background. At sixteen came the first job at New York's Worth's Museum; the dance: *Gavotte d'Amour;* the salary: twenty dollars a week for eleven performances a day. In order to expend some of her excess energy, she took part in a six-day bicycle race in New York and came in sixth; later, in Pennsylvania, she won a state championship.

As a cloak model she practiced dancing in the dressing rooms, and as a ballet dancer she trotted about on toe slippers in *The Ballet Girl,* produced in 1898. Here, on the basis of her three ballet lessons and strenuous practice while clutching the side of the dining-room table, she pirouetted onto the stage, leaped over a balustrade, landed on her knees, executed a few tricks (including a roll-over) and pranced off.

Then came the seasons with David Belasco, who, as she later said, "canonized me" from Ruth Dennis to Ruth St. Denis. As a dancer and a budding actress, she traveled to

Europe and over the United States in support of Mrs. Leslie Carter, and while she was playing Buffalo in *Du Barry*, a production in which she danced and sang, came the incident which changed the course of her life.

The poster did it—a poster advertising Egyptian Deities cigarettes. She saw it in a store window, obtained it and found in it the key which unlocked the treasury of ideas and passions long hidden within her. The poster itself, showing a serene figure of the goddess Isis sitting upon a throne, could not, within itself, have changed the course of a career unless the career had been prepared for change.

Although the poster made the break with the past inevitable, it by no means represented a blueprint of the future. "When I identified myself with the little seated figure of Isis," she said,

> I didn't think at all. My ego, hovering near my solar plexus (maybe!), simply expanded itself into proportions of power and joy within that left me in complete amazement at the whole experience. For you see, in the split second of time after I got the poster home and stuck it up on the wall I said to myself, "Hereafter, I will be Egypt. . . ." Just see how little things like this can change a whole lifetime. No Egyptian dancer stuff for me. Me, bursting out into a whole nation's activities in movement.
>
> Don't ask me why it had to be a new dance form that I should create instead of drama or poetry or painting. I don't know. At that time there was no dance form I could follow. I was born into a world of splits and kicks in vaudeville and a completely moribund ballet at the opera. No food here for my voracious appetite.

With the discovery of the poster, the urge to "dance" Egypt became an obsession. There was no thought of continuing with the theater as she knew it, no desire to capitalize on her initial successes and strive for stardom as either an actress or a dancer in the accepted traditions. She knew that her new work would lead her into untold difficulties, for she had no money for *Egypta,* no public prepared to accept a New Jersey girl who sought for God through dance and very little dance equipment with which to give substance to her impassioned feelings and ideas. She didn't care. The inner compulsion was far too great to be denied, even to be questioned.

For the remainder of the *Du Barry* tour, St. Denis poured over books and photographs dealing with Egypt and slowly the plan of *Egypta* evolved. Back in New York with her family, she continued her study and accepted professional assignments in order to raise money. Finally, it became clear that *Egypta* would be too expensive to produce and that some preliminary dances would have to pave the way for the new work.

A visit to Coney Island brought St. Denis into contact with the Hindu dance as performed by members of an East Indian village on display at Coney. She immediately determined to work out some nautch dances for vaudeville and from the money thus raised to pay for *Egypta,* but research into the nautch matter led her inevitably from the street dances to the temple dances of India and the spirit behind *Egypta* found a different form in *Radha.*

In the first 1906 program, which included *The Incense* and

The Cobras as well as Radha, no attempt was made for ethnic dance authenticity. The mudras, or hand gestures, and the very architecture of the dances suggested the spirit and the colors of Oriental dance rather than reproducing its forms.

The Incense, for example, bore little resemblance to the traditional invocations to the gods of India as far as form and technique were concerned, but an invocation it most certainly was. The stage was bathed in a soft blue light, the figure seemed to emerge from the light itself and the dance was as quiet, as delicate as the background from which it came. The figure quietly crumbled incense into trays of glowing charcoal, touched her hands together in attitudes of supplication, permitted her body to mirror in movement the spirals of smoke. The torso swayed ever so gently, the arms rippled ever upward, culminating, like the smoke of the incense, in a finger pointed heavenward toward deity.

The Cobras, of course, was utterly different. Instead of coolness, shadows and beauty, were heat and blazing sunlight and evil. Here was a harsh-faced being, dirty of dress, ambling into a public square, her snakes lying limp across her shoulders. For the crowd of onlookers she rouses them, permits them to play about her body, wreathe around her neck, coil and dart, their green eyes glittering in the sunlight. She begs for "baksheesh," curses and spits when it is not forthcoming and, tossing the snakes again about her shoulders so that their eyes gleam evilly from her back as she turns away, shuffles off, greasy black hair straggling from her turban. The cobras were St. Denis' arms, their eyes were emerald rings upon her fingers and the movements so revolutionary that, a few years later, a group of doctors in Berlin would study her arm and shoulder actions microscopically, believing that she must be deformed.

Following her first concerts, St. Denis left for Europe and triumph. London liked her; Paris, after an episode involving an impostor calling herself Radha, adored her; and in Germany her triumph was complete. The critics viewed her works seriously, and articles concerning her divulged the philosophical and spiritual aspects of her dancing. In short, she was treated as an artist. She remained in Germany for almost two years, and if she had been willing to make that country her headquarters, a theater would have been built especially for her. But America, home, called, and in 1909 she returned to her native land.

With *The Green Nautch* (the first of several dances in the style of the Indian street dancer) and the highly spiritual *Yogi* added to her repertory, she arrived in America and found, as several artists of the day had discovered, that the accolades of Europe opened American doors to American performers. Europe had acclaimed her, so America decided that she must be good.

Continuing under the management of Henry B. Harris, who had believed in her and had arranged her initial New York tryout, St. Denis was able to create the long-postponed *Egypta*. And, as she had planned, *Egypta* was not merely about an Egyptian dancing girl but about Egypt herself, her heritage and her immortality.

The ballet commenced with "The Invocation to the Nile," in which St. Denis, as the priestess-leader of a group of temple girls, identified herself through her flowing, rippling motions with the life-giving force of Egypt herself, the Nile. Next came the temporal "Palace Dance," followed by the spiritual "Veils of Isis," in which compassion and the promise of resurrection were reflected in the dance of the goddess. In "The Dance of Day," the living and the fighting, the hunting and the building, the arts and crafts of ancient Egypt were suggested in dance, while in the closing episode, "The Dance of Night," Egypta came before the tribunal of the gods in the hall of judgment, bearing her heart in a jar. And when her heart was weighed against the feather of truth, it balanced and Egypta stepped into the boat of Ra, the sun, and was borne to the kingdom of the blessed.

By 1909 newspaper headlines had ceased their strident humor about her, and authoritative critics, although not dance critics (for there were none) , were prepared to discuss her as an artist. Philip Hale, the distinguished music critic, wrote of her in that same year:

> In comparison with the dancing of Ruth St. Denis, the posturing, the prancing, the loping, the bounding of Isadora Duncan seem common and material. It is true that Miss St. Denis has natural advantages over the majority of her sisters in art. She is tall and of entrancing proportions. From the sole of her foot to the crown of her head she is apparently without blemish. Her knees might well have moved the Singer of Solomon's Song to Rapture. The ensemble of her body is as a flawless lyric.
>
> And yet there is this to be said that to some might be paradoxical: although her body is that of a woman divinely planned, there is no atmosphere of sex about her whether she is immovable upon the altar—a picture of

beauty never to be forgotten—or dancing the sense of touch.

Although the return to America ushered in years of artistic success, the struggle continued. *Egypta* was expensive to produce; *O-Mika,* a Japanese dance drama, was not a popular success; excursions into vaudeville were necessary to make ends meet. But by this time her contributions to the world of dance were considerable. She had evolved new ways of movement and rediscovered the profound purposes of dance; together with Isadora, she had influenced fashions in dress, and, with her brother as her stage manager, she had created new lighting effects for the theater.

During this early period of intense creativity and artistic success, St. Denis was torn, as she had been most of her life, by inner conflicts. Had the public understood that she was not merely an "Oriental" dancer but an artist who had selected the Orient's forms to convey her message of man's spirit? Was she on the right track?

At this point in her career, a young man eager in manner and proud of his initial success in transforming himself from a theological student into a dancer came into her life. He applied for a position in her company, was hired and married his hirer in 1914, shortly after their first meeting. His name was Ted Shawn.

Their tender and stormy marriage, which ended (they were never divorced) with their artistic separation in 1931, is a full story in itself. But during their years together they laid the foundations of the American dance through their famed company of Denishawn Dancers, which was to carry their version of dance throughout the nation and to many quarters of the globe, and the Denishawn schools, prepared to bring new forms of dance to thousands of students.

Denishawn meant something different to each of its founders. For St. Denis, Denishawn at its worst seemed to tie her down, to shackle her to the demands of others, to hold her to schedules for weeks and months and years. From time to time she rebelled, left Denishawn entirely in Shawn's hands, but ultimately returned. At its best for her, Denishawn enabled her to produce ideas long dormant in her mind by providing her with money, trained personnel and equipment necessary to large-scale productions.

The tremendous success of Denishawn also made it possible for her to bring her way of dance to larger audiences over broader areas than ever before. The huge earning capacity of Denishawn made possible the staggering expenditures for lavish new works, such as the Babylonian *Ishtar,* and, with the company's Oriental tour in 1926, St. Denis was able to visit for the first time the scenes of her initial inspirations.

In her husband she found new sources of encouragement, stimulation and, perhaps, a discipline which she resented but needed, and in him she also had a partner, a co-artist of extraordinary gifts. Together, they gave the public an exciting array of theater creations, a teaching system which prepared many to carry on the work of extending the range of contemporary dance and several young dance stars, among them Martha Graham, Doris Humphrey and Charles Weidman, who were destined to share in the leadership of a later period of American dance.

With the separation of St. Denis and Shawn, Denishawn as

an institution came to an end. Quietly St. Denis sank into comparative obscurity, emerging occasionally to appear in her historic solos. But she was by no means inactive, not discouraged by financial reverses. A new project was under way. The ideas and the goals of one who always, in her own words, "wanted to dance God" were the same, but the forms were different.

In her new creations she forsook the trappings of the Orient and danced her universal themes of man's kinship with God in terms of the Christian church. The lure of the exotic, the novelty of a new personality and youth were no longer hers, but she persisted and, with the formation of a Rhythmic Choir, she was able to create dances and pageants on Biblical themes for presentation in churches, occasionally in the theater, frequently in little studios.

Finally, in 1947, with Hollywood instead of New York as her headquarters, she established her Church of the Divine Dance where she commenced the building of a dance liturgy suitable to the varied services conducted by guest churchmen, theologists, philosophers.

It would be inaccurate, however, to state that Ruth St. Denis danced nothing but religious themes, for although the majority of her works were of a spiritual nature, nonsacerdotal beauty also evoked the spirit of creation within her. Among dances of this genre one would list *Spirit of the Sea*, in which she manipulated yards of material spread across the stage, her own white hair serving as the foam of the sea. Certain dances evoking the styles of classical Greece were primarily concerned with movement design, and her "music visualization" dances were, of course, without literary or dramatic theme.

An intense patriot, she occasionally directed her choreographic skill toward dances reflective of the spirit of her country. Her *Freedom,* a long solo created in 1955, found her patriotic and religious feelings combined in a work for which she wrote a poetic narrative as co-accompaniment with the musical base. But each one who ever saw her dance in 1906, in 1956, in 1966, or in the years between will remember something different about her.

There are those who will recall the mystic message of *Radha;* others, the writhing arms, the glittering eyes of *The Cobras.* Some will see the sinuous and sensual movements of *Salome* or the sinuous but spiritually sensitive motions of *The Incense.* The walk of the redeemed in *Yogi* cannot be forgotten, and the romantic can hardly erase from his memory the vision of the blue-draped, white-haired figure dancing her moonlit dream of love, *Liebestraum.*

To Ruth St. Denis, each of her dances represented a part of herself, a segment of her spirit. She enjoyed her "historic dances" (a generous number exist in whole or in part on movie film), but she was always the restless creator. In the last decade of her life, religious themes were paramount. She was interested in all religions, and in building her proposed dance liturgy she did elaborate research before creating her ceremonies in dance. She was still exercising and dancing daily, as well as choreographing, teaching and lecturing when she died, after an illness of only a few days, in 1968, at the age of ninety-one.

If she had been asked to name a dance which embodied her spiritual approach to her art, she might have selected the closing passages of her *Color Study of the Madonna*. Here, wearing a cloak of gold, she assumed the crown of the Queen of Heaven and, her face touched with serenity and light, her arms and body lifted upward, reached with gentle ecstasy toward deity.

7

Ted Shawn

Muscles strain against their fetters. A rumor of beauty, borne by the insistent rhythms of music, touches the struggling, sweating body, urges it to greater effort, lends its rhythmic strength to the battle and the bonds fall loose. The figure, freed, stumbles out of the darkness, out of the falseness of shadows into the light. And as the light of truth, the air of freedom greet the newcomer, he sings, not with his voice but with his body. Arms and head upraised in ecstatic gratitude, he moves as only the newly liberated can move, testing the resilience of each muscle, exploring the earth with his feet, discovering new patterns in space, soaring, spinning, stamping, slashing the boundless air with the arc of an arm, with the entire periphery of his moving body.

Then, with arms outspread, with muscles pulling their full length, he poises in a second of suspension, like a bird, motionless but moving through space. And like a bird, he has discipline, the discipline of rhythm and of pattern, a pattern freely traced, if you will, but a pattern in keeping with the laws of movement, of direction, of dynamics, of space.

This light, this air are not for one alone. The figure, refreshed, returns inevitably to the darkness and to the shadows, exhorting those shadows of men to break their bonds and to see the light of truth and to breathe the air of freedom. The exhortations are in vain, for the shadows believe not and understand not. Unhappy, miserable, they know only a world of darkness and of chains, and this gesticulating idiot, this divine idiot convinces them not at all.

He beats his thighs, he points to the path, empathically he tries to help them strain their shackles off. Finally he sees one of the shadow men commence to struggle, to strain against his bonds. His message believed, even by one, he knows that he is free and he rushes back to the light and to the air.

A sermon has been preached, not with words, but with every fiber of the body. Unlike a sermon, however, it is not confined to the inexorable, immutable definition of words. Perhaps it tells of Christ, exhorting the unbeliever to find the Kingdom of God; perhaps it is the philosopher, leading his fellows nearer to the truth; perhaps it is the patriot, fighting for freedom and faith. But it is a sermon and it is a sermon preached with the universal vocabulary of human movement, a magic vocabulary which seems to speak to man in his own tongue. The preacher is Ted Shawn; the dance, for it is a dance, *The Divine Idiot*.

Shawn, whatever else he is, whatever his theatricality, is a preacher. That he forsook the study of theology in his college days did not mean that he forsook the ministry; he simply exchanged the pulpit for the theater, words for action, community service for the world of art.

Like many another artist before him and contemporary with him, he has been a purveyor of joy and of excitement and of romance to the many and a prophet to the few. If the felt but not understood dynamics of *The Divine Idiot* stirred the senses of many an onlooker, if the rapid spins, the rush of action, the pictorial beauty of a body in motion pleased the general public, some, at least, saw the message and others were exposed to it. The sermon was there, it was in a universal tongue, but not everyone had learned to respond to the meanings of motion.

Shawn's ministry of dance was as inevitable as the ministry which any artist, any innovator is compelled, by his inner drive, to follow. The career of a dancing preacher seemed almost predestined. Through his mother, Shawn was related to that great family of actors, the Booths. His home environment was one of sober piety and unshakable faith, a faith enlarged through the friendship of a vital, humorous and understanding Methodist minister. And, finally, his personal composition was rich in energy, determination, avidity for knowledge and latent curiosity.

Strangely enough, it was neither an agile body nor a flair for kinetics which led the young man to dance. It was paralysis. The story of young Ted Shawn's months of paralysis is known to everyone who professes an interest in dance. But it is a good story, for it tells of a youth who, while studying for the ministry, contracted diphtheria and through an overdose of serum was left crippled, and who, through an indomitable will, forced his muscles to move, thereby moving himself out of the ministry and into dance.

Up to the time of his hospitalization, Shawn was, according to his own words, a "yes-man." Provided he respected a tutor, guide or mentor, he agreed with their creeds, their statements. Because he was religious by nature and by upbringing, he accepted the normal route to an actively religious life, and prepared himself for the ministry through additional schooling and study. If his instincts and desires were deep, his thoughts were not, and it required the agony of paralysis, the months of lonely recuperation to govern instinct and desire with careful, probing thought. In the clearinghouse of the hospital, he stopped saying "yes" and commenced to say "why?" "but," "I'm not so sure," "I don't agree" and, finally, "This is the truth." The "truth" he found to be "that thing which I can make work," and he found, perhaps by chance, perhaps through the parallel necessity of making his ailing body work again, that he could make dance work.

In his home city of Denver, he saw, and fell in love with, Ruth St. Denis. On the softly lighted stage moved the figure, her arms raised in supplication, her body reflecting in its motions the gently weaving pattern of smoke borne heavenward from the incense tray. Here were dedication and invocation, here was a dance of prayer. A tall, husky youth saw in it the clue to the kind of dance he sought.

Neither determination nor inner compulsion, by themselves, can make a dancer. Shawn had to master the instrument which was to be the medium of his ministry; secondly, there was no teacher who could train him in the use of that instrument for the purposes he had planned. Initial ballet lessons from a local teacher, Hazel Wallack, strengthened the body-instrument, made it more supple, coordinated its component parts, introduced it to exercises which would, at least, prepare it for further compositions. But ballet, as such, was not for Shawn. Its formalities were not suited to a six-foot frame, and there were no words in its kinetic vocabulary which could be used in the preachments of dance.

Once the basic training was over, the young man could never adhere to any single school of movement. He saw the dance complete, a dance which embodied ritual, physical compulsion, sex motivation, intellectual desire and mimetic communication. He believed that every dance form, every technique could and should be used by the dancer in evolving his own category of motion and that the motor manifestations of the human body could be limited only by the muscular limitations of that body.

Accused of eclecticism, he accepted the derogatory term as a compliment, believing that through the ecstatic spinning of his *Mevlevi Dervish,* through the footbeats of *Thunderbird,* through the gentle plastiques of *St. Francis* or through the personalized movements of *The Divine Idiot* he would provide new manifestations of the deity of man, new avenues for the beholder to pursue in the search for that deity which lay hidden within. Through his eclecticism he was, indeed, searching for a global dance.

The first years of his professional life as a dancer, 1911–1914, permitted no time for the transference of the religious aims of the young theologian to the young dancer. He was too busy assembling dance materials, learning how an American should dance. Not only was he far too big in stature and too large of limb to execute effectively the feet-twittering actions of much of the ballet, but also he was convinced that ballet technique alone could not project the themes of man's behavior and man's search for deity about which he would ultimately dance. Further, the theater was in his blood and he never forsook the laws of the theater in order to reveal the laws of living and of faith.

This theatricalism, which lifted him to a position as America's most popular male dancer, was also the cause for some of the most brutal criticism tossed his way. To some, only his theatricalisms were real, and his subject matter, to them, was deemed false and pretentious. They failed to understand that his theatrical eloquence was parallel to the oratorical eloquence of the successful evangelist, that whether he was purposely or subconsciously theatrical, he was ever sincere in his thematic substance.

Some of his early dances he remembers with nostalgic tolerance, realizing that, good, bad or indifferent, they played their roles in preparing him for his dance maturity. Clutching a dagger, he leaped around in animal skins as a primitive; clutching another dagger, he leaped about as a not quite so feral but genuinely enthusiastic Arab; clutching a bunch of grapes, he gave bacchanalian Greece a whirl; with Egyptian cymbals, a Slavonic sword, the drooping sleeves of a Pierrot and with innumerable other costume and kinetic manifestations of the world's dances, he explored the half-forgotten pathways of dance.

That he stumbled occasionally, that he missed some of the treasures lying along the way and had to return again for more careful search, was inevitable in one who visioned "dance complete," who had no guide to direct him, who had so little time in which to accomplish the mammoth task of building a great portion of that foundation which was to support, in the years to come, the structure of a new American dance.

If religious themes were temporarily cubbyholed, the determination to become an "American" dancer was not. Selection of primitive, Oriental or Spanish dance themes may have appeared as a rather roundabout way to become a strictly American dancer, but the logic was sound and theatrically astute. One way would have been to evolve a body technique with which to dance purely American themes, and this was the approach later dancers were to take. Shawn also worked along this line, particularly in his building of a way of movement for American men, for athletes. But in addition to experimenting with "pure" dance, he felt it necessary to work with ethnic dance forms which, through him, would be metamorphosed into personal dance expressions.

By 1914 the blueprint had been made and the construction of a dance career was under way. There was the will to dance, "to see the dance whole," to be an American dancer, to dance as a man should dance and to evolve a technique which could project the ideas and the ideals of man. Further, a professional career had already got under way with a Ted Shawn School in Los Angeles, a partnership with Norma Gould, a Thomas Edison experimental dance movie (*Dance of the Ages*) made and transcontinental tours accomplished.

In that year of 1914, however, a new era of dance building

began for Shawn, for he met and married his "goddess," the dancing figure who had stirred him with her kinetic invocation, the greatest name in American dance, Ruth St. Denis.

He discovered, ultimately, that he had married not a goddess but a tempestuous, difficult, charming, amusing, brilliant, unpredictable woman. But while he was discovering, within his mind, which qualities outweighed which, and while St. Denis was making her own discoveries and decisions about him, their decade and a half of married life paralleled the richest, busiest and most successful years dance in America had ever seen.

His Los Angeles classes were absorbed by their newly founded Denishawn School, his career was linked with hers, and while the combination of their foibles would one day erupt and destroy their marriage, the combination of their gifts made the greatness of Denishawn possible. It has been said that St. Denis was the spirit and Shawn the form of Denishawn, but it would probably be fairer to say that each placed the stamp of his own concepts, spiritual and functional, on Denishawn. In organizational matters, however, it was Shawn who bore the greater part of the burden, willingly and rightly, since earlier schooling and experience had equipped him for the job.

If Denishawn, both as a school and a company, was often viewed as an onus to St. Denis, to Shawn it meant an opportunity to experiment on a grand scale and to bring fruition to plans long held in abeyance. In the school system, over the years, he was able to introduce a variety of dance styles and techniques and to test his beliefs that this very variety of material was essential to the education of the dancer.

Shawn, of course, brought to Denishawn his own vocabulary of movements, aspects of primitive dance and popular dance and an adapted version of ballet. St. Denis contributed, initially, her knowledge of Oriental dance forms and her own motor discoveries. As the years passed, each learned, discovered and mastered further movement idioms and these too became a part of an ever-expanding curriculum. Various teachers, specialists in certain styles of dance or representatives of arts closely allied with dance, were added to the faculty. For Shawn, then, this signified the beginnings of a dance university and not merely (but that also) a training ground for potential members of the Denishawn company.

As co-choreographer for the company during its initial years, Shawn quite logically bent his creative interests toward those of his wife, whose fame rested mainly, but not entirely, on her Oriental dances. Religious themes were not forgotten, but they were flavored with the lore of Egypt, Greece, India, Arabia, Siam or Japan. This was inevitable while at the same time it was ephemeral. St. Denis had found dance and, with that finding, the path to religion. Shawn had commenced with religion and had found dance. That a great many of their creations, born of spiritual search together, should be couched in the dance languages of the East was only natural, since a new husband and a young partner would have been foolish to insist upon the discarding of the valuable theatrical traditions established by his wife.

Shawn, however, did not neglect Americana or Christian themes. As early as 1917 he presented an entire service in dance form at the International Church in San Francisco, and again and again throughout his career his dance would find sanctuary in a church. But although he was eminently successful in the role of dancer-preacher, he preferred to present his religious dances in the theater. In later years, with his men dancers, Shawn often invited his audience to become a congregation as he brought a program to a close with a strong, simple and noble dance treatment of "The Doxology" (or "Old Hundred").

As for American themes, he turned first to those with ethnic flavors, creating dances and ballets suggested by the lore of the American Indian. In fact, one of his most successful works was *Xochitl,* an Aztec dance tale which starred the young Martha Graham. Later dances dropped the ethnic trappings and concentrated on contemporary America, the American pioneer or America in the abstract, the American "Everyman."

With the separation of Ruth St. Denis and Ted Shawn in 1931 came the end of Denishawn, and Shawn found himself broke (Denishawn had made millions, but everything had gone into new productions), middle-aged and bereft of the accompanying magic of his wife's name. But his career was by no means over. He formed a company of men dancers and began the battle—previously one for himself as a single male —for all men who wanted to dance.

Combing colleges for young and virile athletes, he selected eight young men and created for them a program which no one could deny was masculine. In its initial seasons, accent was placed upon primitive dances, sports suites, dances of warriors, and even nonliteral, non-narrative works were flooded with distinctly male action.

The repertory was shrewdly chosen. Audiences accepted

the stamping feet, the twisting torsos, the incantational qualities of American boys "playing" at being Indians, Maoris, Igorots. Quietly, the audience was led to *Olympiad*. Here they witnessed the lithe grace of the fencers; the shifting bounce, the fistic thrust of the boxer; the high jumps and back flips of the cheerleaders; the speed, the vibrant poise of the steel-limbed track man; the clean-legged run, the swift leaps of the banner bearer. Surely, no one could doubt masculinity here. It was dance, of course, but to the onlooker it was near enough to sports to make it acceptable.

Then there was *Labor Symphony*, a work in which the men in an audience could see themselves, their skills, their strength and their bravery idealized and women saw their husbands as, perhaps, they would like them to be. Brawny arms, callused hands threw the seeds into furrows which had been plowed by the force of straining muscles. Crops were harvested, bales of produce tossed and, finally, the rough and tumble of a game, or call it a dance, when the work was done.

Next came the twist of the body, the lift of the shoulder and the percussive downward sweep of an arm as the ax cut into a tree. And there were also men upon the sea, standing tall in the prow, pitting their strength against the waves, bending their backs and lending their sinews to the onward pull of the oars. Labors on the cleared land, in the forest and on the sea led to the toil of men and machines, and in every area of labor one watched American men. They were dancing, but they were men, for theirs were the actions of men.

Through the programs of Shawn and his men dancers passed a parade of dancing men: the shouting, body-dipping

Maori warriors; American Indians soaring on eagle wings or stamping magic from the earth; gold-panning, high-kicking forty-niners; jug-hunting, coonskin-capped pioneers; soldiers fighting, dying, praying; false-faced, snake-hipped, jazz-mad youngsters and, in one great dance, *Kinetic Molpai,* the men of tomorrow.

It seems to many that with *Kinetic Molpai* Shawn had reached his creative peak in choreographing for the male body. The movements exploited motor possibilities suitable to masculine muscles: the force of oppositions, the forward surge of parallelisms; the feline successions of a body moving in chromatic scale from foot to head, each vertebra stating its own action on the way; resilience, the bounce and rebound of a body thrusting itself away from gravity; movements on the ground, on foot, in the air.

Through its abstract patterns, *Kinetic Molpai* told of the strength, but the futility, of oppositions, of struggle, of man fighting man, but it also revealed the weakness of thoughtless unity, of regimentation. It introduced the figure of love, of brotherhood, and in its apotheosis it made manifest, through its movements, that each individual has his own way of dancing (and of living) , and that he is free to pursue such a course as long as it does not harm or destroy the dancing (or the living) of his neighbor, and, furthermore, that the contributions of each may be absorbed into a unified effort, group action not regimented but ordered, not changeless but constantly growing through the discoveries and accomplishments of the individual. Here, in *Kinetic Molpai,* one could watch a brilliant display of masculine dance action and see, if he chose, a manifesto for democracy.

After seven years, Shawn disbanded his company of men dancers. They had enjoyed enormous success, but they had completed their pioneering duties in establishing the right of American men to dance. Further, Shawn had created just about all he was prepared to create for an ensemble of men, and with World War II on the horizon his dancers would soon be off to serve their country in uniform.

The next phase of the Shawn career found him far less concerned with dancing and choreography (although he kept his hand in both) than with the duties of an impresario, director, teacher, writer.

Jacob's Pillow, his colonial farm near Lee, Massachusetts, had first served as a retreat for a busy artist, then as a training ground for his men dancers and later as a site for summertime dance-festival performances presented in the big studio. By 1942 the Ted Shawn Theater, seating five hundred persons, had been built on the place and the annual Jacob's Pillow Dance Festival had commenced to come into its own.

The development of the Jacob's Pillow Dance Festival and its associated school was as difficult a task as Shawn ever faced. Money for building and expansion was hard to come by, and, during the war years, gas rationing held down the theater's potential income. But with an enthusiastic board of directors behind him, through his own manual efforts as a builder and repairer and because of his indomitable spirit, Shawn managed to keep Jacob's Pillow alive through the war and to preside over its growth in the years which followed.

As impresario, he imported soloists of the Royal Danish Ballet to Jacob's Pillow, and from this exposure came engagements on a national level for the entire Royal Danish Ballet.

(For his services to Denmark Shawn was knighted by King Frederick IX.) Other importations included the Ballet Rambert, England's oldest dance company, the Royal Winnipeg Ballet and the National Ballet of Canada, the Celtic Ballet of Scotland, Britain's Ballet West, as well as artists from India, Ceylon, Samoa, Mexico and elsewhere. He had never neglected American dancers, ballet and modern, famous or beginners, and at the Pillow has presided over the premieres of more than two hundred works, ballet, modern, ethnic, avant-garde, multi-media.

Semiretired in his eightieth year, Shawn has delegated many of his duties to his staff, but he continues as artistic director (or adviser) to the Festival, which attracts about thirty thousand visitors every summer, and he occasionally teaches in the Festival's related school.

The Jacob's Pillow school, which Shawn calls a "university of the dance" (it is not quite that, but the pattern is there), has usually been headed by a distinguished faculty representing many aspects of dance and allied studies. Here again, then, is mirrored Shawn's vision of "the dance complete." And here at Jacob's Pillow is a dance plant providing the perfect dance supervision for a senior artist, for a man with years of pioneering, performing, choreographic, instructional and organizational experience behind him, for a man who always got things done.

Not everything Ted Shawn has done is worthy of praise. Anyone so prolific and opinionated is certain to make mistakes and, although it is as hard for a choreographer to admit that some of his dances are not very good as it is for a mother to admit that one of her children is not very pretty or not quite bright, Shawn can be urged into a grudging admission that some of his efforts were not altogether successful.

He is adamant in his contention, however, that judgment of a creative figure should be based upon his entire output and not upon a single dance or isolated series of works. And if one looks at Ted Shawn in this light, his accomplishments loom large. First of all, he commenced with a body (and an ailing body at that) not suited to the accepted form of the dance of that day, the ballet; second, he was forced to create a movement idiom suitable not only to his own body but also to the body of the average, husky American male; third, he wanted to evolve a dance capable of conveying ideas of the mind and of the spirit, an unheard-of notion prior to Duncan and St. Denis; fourth, he wanted to convince over one hundred million Americans, who did not want to be convinced, that dancing was an honorable profession for real American men; fifth, he strove to bring a concept of "the dance complete" to students and audiences across the nation. That he succeeded in carrying out his aims to a degree beyond his wildest hopes is proof not only of his dauntlessness but also of an aspect of genius.

Whatever has been said of him, truthfully or untruthfully, about his taste (or lack of it), his stature as a great dancer (or merely a proficient one), his choreographic skills (or shrewd theatricality) or any of a number of points disputed by his ardent admirers and his equally ardent critics, no one can deny his powers as a dedicated preacher-dancer. Perhaps his old solo *Prometheus Bound* best describes him, his style, his attitude and his mission.

Upon the stage is an enormous shelf of rock and chained to

that rock is Prometheus. The movements of the figure are circumscribed by the fetters and by the rock itself, yet the actions are heroic.

The anguished twist of the body, the wrenching of the shackles, the arms upraised in plea and in defiance of the heavens are the actions of a hero. The agonies, the tortures of this titan are not only borne, they receive compensation in the knowledge that his gift of fire, symbol of light and warmth and power, now belongs to mankind. From his particular Calvary, he looks down upon man and is content, and with a final effort, he raises himself upright, his body taut, his head thrown back, his arms reaching high, triumphant. A sermon in dance has been preached.

John Durang, eighteenth-century American dancer, a self-portrait. (Courtesy Historical Society of York County)

LA PETITE AUGUSTA.
Aged 10 Years
In the Character of Zoloe in the Bayadere.

Augusta Maywood, nineteenth-century American ballerina, as a child.

Above left, Fanny Elssler in *La Cachucha*. (Courtesy New York Public Library Dance Collection) Above right, Marie Bonfanti, ballerina of *The Black Crook*. (Courtesy New York Public Library Dance Collection) Below, a Shaker religious service. (Courtesy New York Public Library Dance Collection) Left, Jim Crow, minstrel man. (Courtesy New York Public Library Dance Collection)

Anna Pavlova. (Courtesy New York Public Library Dance Collection)

Vaslav Nijinsky in *The Afternoon of a Faun*. (Courtesy New York Public Library Dance Collection)

Adeline Genée, Danish ballerina. (Courtesy New York Public Library Dance Collection)

Drawings of Isadora Duncan by A. Walkowitz.

Ruth St. Denis in *Radha*, 1906. (Apeda)

Ruth St. Denis in *The Yogi*, 1966.

Portrait of Ruth St. Denis. 1964. (John Van Lund)

Ruth St. Denis dancing "The Delirium of the Senses" in *Radha* (1906).

Ruth St. Denis and Ted Shawn at the height of their joint career in *Algerian Dance*.

Ted Shawn, at the start of his career, in a primitive dance.

Ruth St. Denis and Ted Shawn in their famed *Tillers of the Soil*.

Ted Shawn with his Men Dancers in *Kinetic Molpai.*

City Center Joffrey Ballet in Gerald Arpino's
Olympics, a ballet which mirrors Shawn's
pioneering efforts for men dancers.

Martha Graham, at the start of her career (1916), when she was a Denishawn dancer. (White)

Martha Graham, 1970. (Ron Protas)

Martha Graham (Erick Hawkins, background) in *Dark Meadow*.
(Photographed for *Life* by Philippe Halsman © 1947 Time, Inc.)

Doris Humphrey when she was a Denishawn dancer.

Doris Humphrey and the Humphrey-Weidman Company (Charles Weidman, second from right) in *The Shakers*.

Above left, Charles Weidman as a schoolboy (1918) in a home-town version of an Aztec dance, inspired by a Geraldine Farrar movie, *The Woman God Forgot*. Above right, Charles Weidman in his famous solo, *Kinetic Pantomime*. (Thomas Bouchard) Right, Charles Weidman, with Beatrice Seckler, in a scene from his satire on the early movies, *Flickers*. (Louis Melancon)

Above, a scene from Hanya Holm's *Trend*. (Barbara Morgan)

Left, Helen Tamiris, with Daniel Nagrin, in *Liberty Song*.

Lucas Hoving (Iago) , José Limón (Othello) and Betty Jones (Desdemona) in *The Moor's Pavane*. (Arnold Eagle)

Merce Cunningham. (Ron Protas)

Paul Taylor, center, and his company in *Orbs*. (Jack Mitchell)

Louis Falco and Sarah Stackhouse in *Argo*. (Frank Derbas)

Norman Walker, Cora Cahan and Dennis Wayne in *Passage of Angels*. (Jack Mitchell)

The Initiate, with Tim Wengerd and Bill Evans, Repertory Dance Theatre (Utah). Martha Swope)

8

Martha Graham

The blood of ten generations of Americans is her bodily heritage, the "bone of the land" in which she lives provides the skeleton of her dances; inseparable, they live in Martha Graham. Features may change, surface characteristics may vary in different dances, themes may be foreign or universal, but the Puritan blood and the American bone are as irremovable from her dances as they are from her own being.

In *Frontier,* created many years ago, she rebuilt, through the ritual of dance, this heritage of blood and bone upon a stage. She stood, at first, with leg held high and foot firmly planted on the top rail of a fence. At times the hands clasped the raised knee and the head bent forward in contemplation; then the body would commence to turn on its pelvis, the spine straightened pridefully, the head became erect and the eyes searched the line of the horizon.

Sometimes the muscles of the face were set and hard, the body held steel-like in a movement of suspended motion, as

the eyes seemed to look beyond a frontier toward the unknown; again, a smile would flicker across the lips as if the
eyes had seen a vision, a vision of a new land of plenty, a life
of greater richness beyond the frontier, and the body would
yearn forward toward the horizon, almost imperceptibly but
enough to reveal the compulsion to explore.

Suddenly came release as the leg wrenched itself free of the
fence and swept head-high in an ecstasy which spread the
loins, freed the spine and gave generation to an abandoned
dance, a reveling in the strength and freedom of the body, a
kinetic declaration of man the freeborn, the unfettered.

But if the Puritan heritage speaks of freedom, it murmurs
also of discipline, and the figure in (or perhaps the figure of)
Frontier ceased its motor paean to the land and commenced
to add functional purpose to its actions. With fleet, tiny steps,
the feet sped across the stage, describing a great square, a new
tract of land with new boundaries or, perhaps, a new arena
for action of any kind by the individual who has successfully
passed one frontier of life and is ready for the next.

Of course, in the first seasons the work was performed,
there were many who failed to understand *Frontier*. Wasn't
dance supposed to be pretty, or, if it had to be serious,
shouldn't it tell a story with nice pantomimic gestures everyone could understand? Where was that frontier anyway?
There was no backdrop showing mountains and prairies nor
was there even a log cabin on the stage. No one plowed and
no one reaped and nary an Indian was killed.

Time magazine spoke of *Frontier* as "high priestess Martha
Graham and her surrealist fence act," and perhaps *Time* was
right, but in a way its editors never suspected. For Miss

Graham was the priestess, the priestess who tries to explain the unknown, the priestess who gives immortality to non-physical heritage through ritual, the priestess who gives substance and articulation to emotion.

Frontier was not a story, not a representation, but a revelation. No pioneer figure ever moved as Graham moved, no young man or woman about to cross a frontier to career or marriage or discovery ever moved as Graham moved, but in all instances the impulses were the same. Contemplation may occur in the brain, release in the heart, discipline in the conscience, but with the dancer they must be permitted to pervade the body and speak through the body so that release of the spirit is made manifest through the joyous movements of dance, or discipline is given overt form through the bearing and actions of the body.

All these inner stimuli, these locked impulses are released by the dancer and are allowed to rush through the being and come to vibrant fulfillment in motion. Then, through the tools of art (or by the priestess), they are given form and pattern and accent, distilled into a theater piece, exaggerated and exalted into a work of art, and a "frontier" is born, the kind of frontier everyone should understand, if not with his mind, then with his senses. Such a frontier speaks not only to the land pioneer but to the pioneer in each man who sometime in his life must cross the threshold from the safe known, past the frontier, to an unsafe but, perhaps, rewarding unknown.

Years of preparation lay behind *Frontier* and those other great Graham works which sought to objectify in physical form the beliefs of mankind as experienced by the dancer herself. There must always have been the compulsion to dance, and, more than that, the seeds of nonconformity must have been present. But first came the need to dance, to dance anything for anyone for no other reason than that a young girl simply had to move.

There are, inevitably, stories of a baby girl who, uninvited, contributed to a church service by dancing in the aisles and who later discovered a whole new plane of life on the elevated platform of a Punch and Judy theater. Another little story, however, may explain even more. The child's father, a physician, convinced his daughter that he knew when she was telling a fib because her muscles, her body, gave her away. Perhaps it was this tiny detail, planted like a new seed in a fertile mind, that made a mature Graham believe not only that dance could encompass the behavior patterns of man but that it could also reveal the nature of man himself.

The early years in Pennsylvania, the place of her birth, the later childhood and adolescence in California saw this innate compulsion to dance throb into full determination to make dancing a lifework. Finally, in 1916, a shy high-school girl slipped through the doors of the Denishawn School in Los Angeles and into the world of dance.

Where to place this new citizen of a dance realm? Its reigning monarchs were undecided. St. Denis, reflecting upon the coming of young Martha to the school, reports that she was somewhat at a loss to know what to do for or with the strange and vivid youngster. Her intense little body did not seem suited to the flowing motions, the delicate gestures which emanated from the long, lithe body of St. Denis.

Shawn was called into conference, and it was decided that

the newcomer must be turned loose in the treasury of Denishawn techniques, where she would find, they hoped, a treasure suited to whatever latent gifts she possessed.

They watched the training process with interest and with concern and were rewarded one day when, through the shy shell of the girl, there burst forth a flame of action. Ballet had not fanned the flame nor had the gentle spirituality of Hindu dance breathed the embers of Martha's dance to life. It was primitive dance which had done it, the primitive dance which sprang from "the bone of the land," which urged the doer to stamp magic from the earth itself, which permitted the dancer to "objectify in physical form" the beliefs, the feelings of the inner man.

There was, at this time, no compulsion to create new dances, new rituals to whatever gods she worshiped. It was enough to be just a dancer, bewildered, bewitched and adoring, and the object of adoration was, of course, Ruth St. Denis. "Miss Ruth," says Martha Graham, "opened a door and I saw into a life."

Those who remember Martha Graham's dancing during her Denishawn sojourn from 1916 to 1923 recall her as a quiet, hard-working student and a performer of vivid gifts. "Abandon" is a word which her Denishawn colleagues frequently used in describing her way of dancing, as if she lost herself and her identity in the patterns of dance. In *Serenata Morisca,* an Oriental dance, and as the maiden in the Aztec ballet *Xochitl,* she achieved nationwide success. Certainly there was abandon in her enactment of the girl in *Xochitl,* for Ted Shawn, often her partner in this ballet, maintained that at the end of a tour he would be bruised and bleeding from the pummelings, scratchings and bitings he suffered at the hands of a girl who protected her honor even against the desires of her emperor. In fairness, it might also be noted that Graham felt that Shawn was fairly abandoned too. "He dropped me on my head once in *Xochitl*," she reports.

After years of performing with Denishawn in Egyptian, Hindu, Spanish, Indian and other dances, Martha Graham's adolescent urge to dance just for the sake of moving was spent. The acolyte had outgrown her religious shell, new deities had to be found, a new tract of dancing explored.

There was no sudden break with the traditions of the immediate past, no hustling up of a new technique overnight, no conquest of a new world of motion as the doors of Denishawn shut behind her. The next step was a time step, marking time, as she joined the *Greenwich Village Follies* as a solo dancer for a two-year stint. But the assignment not only gave her time to think about the next step; it also supplied her with money, enough money to make possible a complete break with the past.

A laboratory was now essential and she found one at the Eastman School of Music in Rochester, New York, where she obtained a position on the teaching staff. Here was an opportunity to test the very chemistries of her being, to fuse them, if possible, into a new element of dance.

Her debut in New York in 1926 as an independent dancer-choreographer provided merely a hint of the Graham to come. The dances were all of her own devising, many of them stressing an aspect of dance which she was later to abandon but one which, in the past, had not been her particular forte. This aspect was concerned with the pictorial and a lyrical form of the pictorial. The press, which in a few years would call her movements "stark" and "ugly," found her gentle, graceful and skilled at making pretty pictures.

One can assume that Martha Graham had no particular desire to be of the pictorial-lyrical school, but perhaps she had to prove to herself that this area of dance was not beyond her reach, or perhaps it was something of a tribute to (and a defiance of) her goddess, Ruth St. Denis, whose lyricism was unmatched and whose genius for creating pictorial movement was legend.

The initial program, April 18, 1926, at New York City's Forty-eighth Street Theater, listed such titles as *Maid with the Flaxen Hair, Clair de Lune, Désir, A Study in Lacquer* and *Three Gopi Maidens.* Negation had not commenced nor had affirmation, but the creative processes were beginning to flow.

Graham was not yet conscious of the forms which her creative compulsions would ultimately generate. She was conscious of nothing but freedom, concerned with nothing but freeing herself from the bonds of the past. Like anyone with newly found liberty, she was not quite certain what to do with it. Artistically, she was at the frontier which separates adolescence from maturity, the known from the unknown. As in her later dance, *Frontier,* she was clinging to the seasoned supports of the past and looking toward the horizon. She was not yet quite ready to wrench the leg free from the fence and dance forward, unfettered, into a new realm of dance.

At Eastman, she continued her experiments. By degrees, she discovered those truths which were to guide her dancing, truths about the architecture of her body, the function of her body, the purpose of her body, each as they related to dance. Since dance and architecture were the primal arts, she knew that she must rediscover their basic associations, and to that end she studied the architecture of her body.

Once she became certain of the architectural properties of her body, she tested the functions of that body and what that body could do within the framework of its own structure. Degrees of expansion and contraction, generated by body energy, were tested; the hinges, or joints, of the body could open up new vistas of movement; in fact, she discovered that a vast area of freedom existed within the structure of the body and that the structure was not so much inhibitive as it was disciplinary, that it governed, rather than curtailed, functions.

Finally, she discovered the purpose of her body: "to objectify in physical form my beliefs." She had come to understand the structure of her body, that it did not imprison her but that it housed her; she had learned what body functions were possible, permissible and in keeping with the architecture of her bones and joint and sinews; and she had found her mission. Once these truths were discovered, there could be no going back, no digressions.

She could no longer dance as others had danced or as others had taught her to dance, nor could she give audiences movements they liked to watch simply because they wanted them. She did not wish to alienate an audience nor did she want to exist without a following, but, like a prophet or messiah, she felt compelled to dance the truth as she saw it. Many would misunderstand, a few would recognize her aims, but she would have to be content with a few. Later, perhaps, others would become converted as they came to respect her determination and as she herself became more articulate in the statement of her principles.

A few seasons after the debut, nothing was left of the pictorial dancer and little of lyricism remained. In their place was percussive vigor, for here was a dancer who attacked a phrase rather than drifting into it, who found the bitter and the biting of more concern thematically than girls with flaxen hair or the activities of Tanagra figurines. The Oriental shell was gone, revealing the descendant of a Puritan, but a Puritan who permitted her passions, in this twentieth century, to break forth and the voice of her own truth to speak out in such dances as *Revolt, Immigrant, Four Insincerities* and *Heretic*.

During this richly creative period from the late 1920's to the late 1930's, she found the need not only to decry and negate but also to affirm, and her affirmations took her along two parallel paths. The first led her to reaffirm the dance heritages of the race of man; the second to affirm the universal, timeless experiences of man. The former caused her to create *Two Primitive Canticles, Primitive Mysteries, Ceremonials* and a host of other works pertaining to the ritual dance and the need of such ritual as "a means of grace and for the hope of glory" for all men of all times.

The second pathway led her to create such kinetic definitions as *Lamentation, Imperial Gesture, Frontier* and supplementary portions of other dances in which she was concerned not with stock gesture, not with indication, but with distillation. *Frontier,* as has been noted, was not a geographical frontier at a given latitude and longitude but was simply a

THE DANCE IN AMERICA

distillation of all the emotions and meanings which the word itself implies.

Lamentation was in the same category as *Frontier*. Here was no mother weeping over a child nor a girl crying over a torn party dress (although it could pertain to both), but the stuff of lamentation itself. Specific stimulus was not revealed, for if it had been, the dance would have meant something only to those who themselves had experienced a similar stimulus—not everyone has lost a child and not everyone has torn a party dress, but everyone has lamented something at one time or another.

Here, then, in *Lamentation,* was a figure contracted in agony, seeking unconsciously the safe position of the fetus, pulled and twisted by visceral pains of anguish, letting the body rack itself in self-flagellation, pushing the feet into the floor, looking and reaching up to escape or to God, shrouded in the confining fabric of sorrow. And each who saw this ritual of lamentation could apply it to himself and to his own experiences, for this was not a case history but, rather, an objectifying in physical form of the lamentations of all men.

The decade from 1928 to 1938, filled as it was with great Graham works, was still a testing period as far as the dancer herself was concerned. Viewing it in retrospect, she refers to it as "the period of long woolens" and admits she wonders why so many of her audiences stood by her. Hard as it may have been on the public in general, it was a necessary period and a vital one. Frequent drabness of dress (the long woolens) and paucity of décor were essential to an artist in quest of the unglossed virtues of dance, and, certainly, stern and serious themes could not bow to levity and lightness in one determined to objectify in physical form her beliefs.

In 1938, with the production of *American Document*, a real high priestess was ordained. With it and subsequent creations, the freeborn artist was apparent. Costuming which augmented dance action, décor which served the choreography and, yes, even pictorial effects, tender romance and speech were permitted to take part in this art effort.

At last Martha Graham knew that her trained, disciplined body could not lie and that whatever it required in the way of support and embellishment was right. Nor was it necessary to deny any longer the heritage of the immediate past, and thus certain applicable qualities of the Denishawn period, of ballet, of drama, of poetry contributed their bits to the Graham dance. As her pioneer ancestors had done before her, Graham had simply cleared the land, planted it with her own seed and then discovered that some of the previous crop, when the tares were removed, could be encouraged to grow again and enrich the produce of her land, of her area of dance.

In quick succession, the years brought forth an array of Graham masterpieces, almost all of them group works. *American Document* was a distillation of the myriad forces which characterize America, forces of good and evil, of activity and passiveness. In *Every Soul Is a Circus* and *Punch and the Judy,* Graham turned to cutting comedy, to biting satire on a woman (*Circus*) who wished to be queen of all she surveyed and a wife (the *Judy*) who fled from reality and responsibility into a happy dream world.

93

There was *Salem Shore,* with its New England housewife waiting on the beach for her husband's return from the sea, her spine straight, her discipline breaking only in the nervous plucking of her skirt. And there was *Herodiade,* terrified of her unknown destiny, preparing for it sometimes with forthright vigor and again with neurotic despair.

New England spoke again in *Letter to the World* through the overt actions of the figure of Emily Dickinson and through the disclosures of the poetess' passionate inner spirit as mirrored in the actions of another figure, the figure of the secret self. The Brontë sisters rushed toward their doom, beset by madness and fear, in *Deaths and Entrances.* The sweet formalities, the reserved affections, the clasp of hands in friendship and hands cupped in prayer to God, the joyousness of folk dance, the love of hearth and the pull of adventure transformed *Appalachian Spring* into an action portrait of America.

Later came *Dark Meadow,* a manifesto to the immortality of man; *Cave of the Heart,* based upon the legend of Medea, a vivid lesson of the death and destruction which are the ashes of consuming jealousy; *Errand into the Maze,* deriving from the classical story of the Labyrinth and the Minotaur but dealing with man's need to do battle with the creature of fear which travels the corridors of his own heart; *Night Journey,* also stemming from classical Greek sources but presenting Jocasta at that moment when she is about to kill herself and the enormity of her tragedy races across her mind.

The classical Greek sources continued to inspire Graham: *Phaedra, Circe, Alcestis* and the first full-length work (four acts) ever done in modern dance, *Clytemnestra,* with a score by the Egyptian composer, Halim El-Dabh. Mention should also be made of *Judith,* a heroic symphonic solo about the Biblical heroine; *Diversion of Angels,* a group work; *Canticle for Innocent Comedians,* another piece for the Graham company in praise of nature; *Part Real, Part Dream,* a dance fantasy; a piece based on the theme of Héloïse and Abelard; a reworking of *Judith* into a full-company work; and the comedy, *Acrobats of God,* in which the dancers themselves are "divine athletes," ever subject to the whip of the task-master who demands perfection of them.

Taking two Graham works for analysis, one finds that they are themselves analyses of their stated themes. Remember two of the basic Graham creeds: "to objectify in physical form my beliefs" and "to reveal the inner man." If these approaches seem esoteric, mystical, a cold look at them discloses their essential rightness. Why objectify something that already has physical object? Let us give substance to beliefs. How can one reveal the outer man when he already stands revealed before the eyes? Let us reveal the inner man in order that we may know not the vehicle but its occupant. In *Appalachian Spring* and in *Dark Meadow* Martha Graham has both objectified and revealed.

The characters of *Appalachian Spring* tell of themselves, of their relationships, of America. The wife (orginally danced by Graham) is reserved in the eyes of her neighbors, but we are permitted to see her inner self. As she sits quietly rocking, we know of her contentment; as she presses herself with violence on the ground, we learn of her love for the soil; as she dances a jig about the stage, her inner joy is made manifest; and in the erectness of her walk, the vigor of her actions, the rebound from anguish to joy, the visceral serenity of repose, we see the indomitable character of the settler.

In the restless, sweeping action of another character in *Appalachian Spring,* the pioneer woman, in her tense attack on whatever she does, through her muscular harangues, we view the woman who not only followed but urged or led her man across the frontiers of a new world.

With the clicking of heels in the air, a physical display of inner bravado, one aspect of the husband is revealed, while the decorum apparent when he speaks to his neighbors tells of his inner solidness, and, finally, the laying of a hand on his wife's shoulder and the gentleness of his glance disclose an inarticulate but very real love. And their dance together, not a folk dance within a ballet but a gay and secret union of movement, gives action-symbol to the passion of their married love.

Movements narrow in dimension, direct and forthright; moments of suspended actions, heroic in repose, delineate the man of God, the revivalist of *Appalachian Spring.* When he soars from the earth in mighty jumps, he is not undergoing a personal ascension but rather is he inviting his congregation to take note of the direction from which will come blessing or punishment. Indeed, in the darting gestures of his arms we can see the warning that Jehovah's thunderbolts will strike the wicked.

Above and beyond the patterns of motion which reveal the individual are those greater patterns which govern the whole assemblage, impelling its members together and apart, drawing the designs of a way and of a period of life, evoking the sweetness of an "Appalachian spring."

Dark Meadow, in effect, is the legend of Isis and Osiris, the New Testament, the cosmic dance of Shiva, Mohammed's promise of heaven, or any and all statements of belief in the life everlasting. It detracts in no way from accepted testaments of faith; in fact, it leans upon them for support and plants its roots in the rich soil of tradition.

Man cannot believe in his mortality, and he must, if his brief span on earth is not to seem futile, find proof that he is eternal; and in *Dark Meadow* Graham dances a role which is all of us. She experiences the agony of loss and seeks proof that her experience was not actually one of loss but of change. Her first proof of immortality comes with an awareness of the "ancestral footsteps" reminding her that if there was an "ago" there must be a "to-come."

For these ancestral footsteps, Graham has created a ritual archaic in flavor but nonracial and of no specific period. It is a ritual for men and women, and it contains a processional, unhurried and serene, a quiet love dance symbolic of physical union, and it magically suggests within its simple pattern that it has been danced forever and that it will continue to be danced into eternity. These are the ancestral footsteps echoing into the future.

Proof of immortality is also found by the seeker in love, in procreation; for through the compulsion of sex, immortality is achieved, an immortality which cannot be hoarded but which can be bequeathed.

In nature, the seeker finds proof of immortality as Persephone comes to clothe, each spring, a barren earth with a mantle of green. But beyond the truth of the past, beyond the law of sex and beyond the miracle of the seasons, the seeker finds belief in the immortality of the spirit through the symbol of the Cross and through those other symbols which promise men of many faiths the same life everlasting.

The greatness of *Dark Meadow* lies not alone in the compelling beauty of its patterns of dance or in the soothing solace which emanates from a ritual of faith but, rather, in its juxtaposition of the fear of death with the actual quest for immortality.

With *Dark Meadow* and the other Graham creations which stir and disturb and illumine, what kind of a theater has Martha Graham built? She herself says that she is striving to build a new pantheon, not of stone or of steel, but a pantheon of the human heart. She believes that "a new mythology must be born, telling of gods and of demons," in order that mankind may be guided anew. Through her "revelation of the inner man," she hopes to add her gods and demons—the gods of love and faith and courage, the demons of hate and jealousy and fear—to this new pantheon and through her "objectifying in physical form my beliefs," she is endeavoring to participate in the creation of a new mythology.

To some, this talk of pantheons and new mythologies is indicative of madness; to others, it suggests the genius. And of genius Graham says, "An insane person is locked up, but a genius is permitted to be mad and live in a conventional society." If Martha Graham is mad, it is because she has found something of madness in her explorations of the nature of man, and if nonmadness is convention, only the mad could create a new mythology to deposit in the pantheon of the human heart. Such madness, such genius is, perhaps, the richest gift that man can offer his fellow men.

In 1971, at seventy-seven, Graham is no longer a dancer. On rare occasions, she illumines the stage with her presence, but her theater and her pantheon and her revelation of man himself continue, vibrantly, with the dancers she has selected to follow her.

9

Doris Humphrey

The reflection in the mirror is utterly still. Then the body begins to sway slightly, away from erectness, only to be drawn back into place by the gentle insistence of muscles. The second sway is in a greater arc, and this time the fibers of the body, instinctively seeking to protect themselves from possible harm, grasp the structure and pull it back to balance.

Another flood of energy propels the body at increasing speed away from its secure axis of balance toward an unknown and dangerous destiny, and sinew must pull against sinew in a tug of war between the instinct for preservation and the urge for adventure. Again the body swings away from its carefully achieved balance and with stepped-up pace and mounting tension rushes through a lawless limbo, governed by neither equilibrium nor gravity, into the domain of gravity and crashes to sudden inaction.

The "arc between two deaths" has been run, the path from inaction to destruction has been traversed. In the mirror, man has seen the ordained range of his physical life, the dramatic possibilities of his emotional life, the path of philosophy clearly marked with the milestones of do-nothing, simple testing, exploration, adventure, madness.

Moving in front of this mirror, Doris Humphrey discovered not only herself but also the stuff of dance. Her discovery was a momentous one, for although the principle was basic, its direct and conscious application to dance was new. Between balance and unbalance, fall and recovery, lay the scope of all human movement. A simple step, even a gesture, threw the body off balance, and certain compensatory movements, some conscious and others instinctive, occurred to restore the balance. The further the body departed from its equilibrium, the greater the compensatory movements had to be.

Inherent in this action were rhythm, drama, idea. Through this principle, dance found its rhythm not in music, not in the pulses of an outer nature, but in the body itself. The seed of drama rested in the dynamic intensities of this principle, and idea became objectified in the degrees to which the dancer permitted himself to depart from balance. The discovery of this principle freed the dancer of dependence upon the other arts, yet it provided him with a dance range of limitless possibilities.

From this swing and sway, this balance and unbalance, this fall and recovery tested in front of a mirror, sprang some of the greatest dance works ever produced in America: the great trilogy, *Theater Piece, With My Red Fires, New Dance; Inquest, Passacaglia, The Shakers*. Here, in this principle of movement, was established a way of dance rather than a crystallized technique, thus enabling each dance creator to employ balance and unbalance as he wished.

Long before the discovery of a new dance principle, there had been years of traditional dance studies and a distinguished dancing career. When she was only eight years old, Doris Humphrey loved dancing and found it easy; in fact, her interest in it was due to the ease with which she mastered her lessons. Under a variety of teachers, she studied ballroom dance, clog, folk, "aesthetic," "interpretive" and classical ballet. But if dancing was easy for her and natural to her, it was also fun, and, in time, she came to discover that she belonged to dance and dance belonged to her.

Following her graduation from high school, young Doris filled her days with further study, with teaching in her home town of Oak Park, Illinois, and with conducting dance classes for summer schools. Then, in 1917, she set forth for California and Denishawn, for a decade of experience, professional growth and resounding success.

At first, Denishawn was "thrilling beyond words," for here the young dancer found "theater, art, life" and discovered that she could be a successful artist-dancer. For five or six years she was able to forget her Middle West background and her New England heritage in the excitement of exotic theater.

By turns, she helped interpret the dance flavors of the Hindu, the Siamese, the Japanese and other peoples of the world and, upon occasion, dance such nonethnic themes as her popular *Hoop Dance*. Her slim beauty, her delicacy of movement, the easy rhythmic pulse which rippled through her body marked her as a lyric dancer, and this lyricism contributed much to the success of Denishawn.

The Denishawn organization also provided her with a unique opportunity to experiment with choreography and in this she was fortunate, for few if any other dance companies of the day would have permitted a youngster to try out her ideas and bring those ideas to fruition in production. One of her creations, *Tragica,* emerged with such completeness of form and with such communicable motor rhythm that the music upon which it was originally built was withdrawn and *Tragica* was then performed without accompaniment, the first dance in contemporary times to stand alone, without a musical crutch, as an example of the independent art of dancing.

In spite of the opportunities for choreographic experimentation and for professional dancing which Denishawn provided Humphrey, and in spite of the native dance genius she gave to the mother company, there was a flaw in the association. As she commenced to grow up and become a mature artist, it seemed to her that it was wrong to be a part of an interpretive idea of presenting the world's people in dance. She realized that she was not really good at being an Indian or a Japanese, and the conviction grew that she would like to be herself.

The smolderings of unrest burst into the flame of revolt following the Denishawn tour of the Orient, for there she discovered what seemed to her to be a discrepancy between the Denishawn Oriental and the real Oriental, between an interpretive dance and the pure ethnologic dance. It became apparent to her that it would be impossible for her as an American to maintain ethnologic integrity in her dancing of Oriental themes, and with that awareness the break with Denishawn was ordained. She was determined to turn toward *her* soil, *her* background and *her* experience for the inspiration and the stuff of her dance.

Following the bitter break with Denishawn, Doris Humphrey and her new partner, Charles Weidman, a principal dancer in Denishawn, set out with their accumulated ideas, hopes and initial experimentations to establish a school and company of their own. It had not been an easy decision to make, and Humphrey soon discovered that it was one thing to reject for herself the ethnologic dances of alien peoples and quite another thing to find just what dance it was which was rooted in *her* soil, *her* background and *her* experience.

There was no basic folk form in America from which she could work, for she was neither an American Indian nor a black American. Furthermore, she felt that the folk patterns transplanted from England, Germany and other countries which mothered American settlers were not actually true representatives of a native and basic folk dance. There was nothing for her to do but create a form without a previously constructed ethnic base, a task spiked with difficulties more numerous than a dance creator would probably find anywhere else in the world.

When Doris Humphrey started working before her mirror, she was in search of something without ethnologic flavor, in quest of the ways in which bodies inherently move before those movements are expanded into styles of dance or patterns of ethnologic action. In the "arc between two deaths," between balance and unbalance, between fall and recovery, she found her answer. If each end of the arc marked the sphere of death, the arc itself represented the dance of life, a nonethnologic, pure dance which could be colored with the rich hues of *her* soil, *her* background, *her* experience.

During the first seasons of independence and continuing exploration, Humphrey created *Color Harmony, Water Study, Life of the Bee, The Drama of Motion, Circular Descent, Pointed Ascent, Dionysiaques, The Shakers* (for a Broadway show) and other works. In these she not only tested the choreographic possibilities of her fall-and-recovery principle, but she also continued her experiments with accompaniment. One dance was soundless except for the movement of dancing bodies, another had music composed after the dance was finished; *Life of the Bee* had a buzzing background, and *The Shakers* was supported by the human voice, drum and accordion.

As her continued development and refinement of the balance-and-unbalance principle led her ever nearer to dramatic forms, Humphrey suddenly realized that she had been adding to some of her dance works movements which had little or nothing to do with her basic principle. These movements, at first used instinctively, she ultimately recognized as belonging to the field of gesture, and she commenced immediately to explore this area of action.

She searched for the meanings of gestures in their long associations in the minds of men, and she used gesture pur-

posely and purposefully in conjunction with dance movement itself in order to achieve the fullest measure of dramatic
communication. If her dramatic movements born of the
balance-and-unbalance principle were almost biological in
nature and were communicated to the audience through
sensory channels, the gestural movements carried their dramatic messages through memory channels to the mind and
from there to the senses.

The addition of gesture to Humphrey's dance by no means
countenanced a return of dance to pantomime, for gesture
was not permitted to take the place of dance. It was fused
with it and made to serve it. In one instance, for example, a
dramatic effect might be gained by the body swinging itself
away from the center of balance in a movement resembling
bowing, but it would not be a formal bow because accent and
motor inflection would be placed upon the general action of
the body. At another time, a gestural bow would be used for
dramatic effect to convey the specific idea of obeisance. By
the former way she gained dramatic communication through
human instinct, while through the latter route, the gestural
way, she made dramatic contact through social memory.

Let it not be supposed that the principle of fall and recovery was immediately discernible to the untrained eye or
that applied gestures stood out like sore thumbs in a given
piece of choreography. The audience was simply aware of the
results of these principles of movement. Audiences, certainly,
did not watch Humphrey and her dancers alternately fall and
recover endlessly and rest for a moment or two on a pattern
of gesture, but they did watch a dramatic thread unspool and
they did react, even viscerally, to the dynamic impulses

emanating from dancing bodies. The techniques, the tools, did not concern them.

In creating a dance, the tools, of course, do not come first. Before they are put to use in building a theater piece, the artist has to have some purpose in mind, a reason for creation. With Humphrey, the stimuli were many. She responded to music, color, drama, movement, literature and idea.

In *Circular Descent* the stimulus was a motor one predicated upon the body's instinctive impulse, when weary, to sink ever downward toward ultimate rest. One of her earliest works, *Color Harmony,* was inspired by a theory of light which she had come across, and a much later work, created for José Limón and his company, was instigated by a poem of García Lorca and by the dramatic implications of the poem itself.

But if she received stimuli from many sources, Doris Humphrey was mainly concerned with ideas, for she believed that ideas were as important as form. "A great abstract dance is not as important as a dance with a deeply moving theme," she said, and coming from one who created perhaps the finest modern-dance abstractions of our time, this seems a strange comment. Yet the fact that she found "beautiful movement is not enough" does not mean that beautiful movement and superb form do not appear in her dances with deeply moving themes.

Her trilogy—*Theater Piece, With My Red Fires, New Dance*—was a work based upon ideas, upon her views of the evils of modern life, of possessive love, of the ideal life—a testament to democracy. In *Inquest* she was fighting injustice; in *Story of Mankind* she was, through brilliant and ironic humor, warning mankind of the dangers of a life based on material benefits alone; and in *Lament for Ignacio Sanchez Mejías* she cried out, through the motions of dance, the message of courage and the hope of immortality.

Even in her bitterest moments, even in the terrifying and searing passages dealing with the destructive love which motivates *With My Red Fires,* she was not "a horrid, grim sadist." She once said, "At heart, I am really a reformer," not a reformer concerned with stamping out but a reformer dedicated to the task of building up that which is fine and right.

"For my part," she said, "every work is colored by the personality of its creator, yet the themes which interest me are tinged with the universal." And although the theme might be basically a personal one, derived from the experience or the observation of the individual and colored by his own character and outlook, it must relate clearly and directly to the experience of others and be of interest and potential concern to them.

In *Circular Descent,* for example, Humphrey was giving dance substance to a personal idea, to the desire she at times experienced to permit her body to sink into the restful earth and to halt the endless battle against gravity, against all opposition. But although the idea of this dance solo was personal to a degree, it pertained to a common instinct and thus was "tinged with the universal."

The same personal-universal tinge may be found in her *Day on Earth* (created for the Limón company) with its themes of labor and play, light romance and profound love, anguish and hope, death and renewal, communicated through the actions of a simple family; or in *Night Spell* (also for Limón), in which a dreamer, like all dreamers, finds the unlikely believable, the desirable elusive, the thrust of nightmare frightening and visions of beauty maddeningly remote.

The choreographic invention of Doris Humphrey spanned more than three decades, continuing long beyond her dancing career, which came to an end in the early 1940's because of a painful and incurable (for dance purposes) hip injury. And during this extended period of dance service she fought innumerable obstacles, in addition to ill health, indomitably, with no pause in creativity. She died in 1958.

The Humphrey-Weidman Company never had easy going. Because modern dance in the 1930's had few followers outside New York and among college students, bookings were hard to obtain and the costs of New York appearances were always higher than the possible proceeds. The dancers' faith in Miss Humphrey and Mr. Weidman and their love of dance held the company together for more than a decade of work, occasionally in New York theaters, sometimes on tour, infrequently in Broadway shows for which the leaders did the choreography and often in studio recitals. With the aid of summertime duties at the Bennington Dance Festival (at Bennington College in Vermont) and teaching jobs, the Humphrey-Weidman Company was able to function.

With her retirement as a dancer, Humphrey turned her full energies and resources to choreography and to direction. As Weidman continued to dance with his own company in his own works, Humphrey assumed the post of artistic director and chief choreographer for José Limón, who had been a soloist with the Humphrey-Weidman troupe and who had come out of his service period in World War II determined to build a career and a company of his own.

Under Humphrey's guidance, Limón emerged as the most vital and distinguished male dancer in the modern field. She guided him, encouraged him to choreograph and contributed to his growing repertory a number of masterful theater pieces which not only exploited his particular talents but also enhanced the prestige of modern dance itself.

Among the Humphrey creations for Limón were the *Lament for Ignacio Sanchez Mejias, Day on Earth, Night Spell; Invention,* a striking, non-narrative dance study; *Ritmo Jondo,* a stirring, pulsating, Spanish-flavored piece depicting the virility of men, the gentleness and quiet bravery of women and the sweetness of union; and *Ruins and Visions,* in which the drama of life and the drama of theater were juxtaposed and interwoven with irony and tender understanding.

In her decade of immeasurably valuable service to Limón and in those supplementary activities which included teaching, the conducting of repertory classes, the directing of workshop units in great works from her vast choreographic output and in newly created pieces, advising dancers who sought her help and giving her time to all causes which furthered the art of dance, Doris Humphrey remained a powerful force on the American dance scene until her death.

In the final months of her life, she completed a long-planned and often-postponed project, the writing of a book on choreography. She literally finished it on her deathbed. It was *The Art of Making Dances,* and was published posthumously in 1959.* It has been considered one of the few truly great books on choreography ever written.

Her skill as a craftsman, her movement inventiveness, her reformer aspect, her search for the universal, her concept of American-rooted dance were mirrored in many of her creations. One of her most enduring and admired choreographies is the García Lorca *Lament for Ignacio Sanchez Mejías*, and perhaps this dance piece, as much as any other of her works, reveals the dance nature of this remarkable woman.

In the *Lament* she fused movements and speech into the drama of dance. The characters are few: Ignacio, Destiny and Woman. Ignacio, though a bullfighter, moves as all men must move through a pattern of life, touching glory briefly, hoping for success, living with more dignity than many men experience and dying with greater courage and richer drama than come to most but dying inevitably as all men die.

The figure of Destiny, the form of a heroic woman, motivates him, spreads the choreographic pathways of life before him, prods him to traverse them, guides him to danger or beauty or love, to living or to death, all with implacable resolve. The figure moves with strength and definitude, touched by neither cruelty nor compassion but with inevitability. She is not a sorceress of the soul; although she plots the courses to be followed, she cannot determine what manner they will be traveled, for it is Ignacio's task to accept love if he so desires, to step with dignity, to live with courage, to face death with serenity.

And Woman. It is she who laments the death of Ignacio, it

* New York, Holt, Rinehart & Winston, 1959.

is she who defies Destiny and it is she who triumphs over Destiny's final pattern of death. Through her lament and her elegy of words and movement, she resurrects the dead and gives him immortality in herself. Her memories bring back the shadows of his actions when living and her love embodies those shadows with new substance and being. Ignacio, free of Destiny, moves again in the heart of one who loved him. Beneath the flaming cape, under the alert and graceful movement of the bullfighter, is man. Ignacio's Destiny is each man's destiny and Woman is each man's loved one.

In *Lament* the poet speaks through action as well as speech. Inner muscles expand and contract the bellows of the lungs and sounds come forth as words of passion born of dance. They speak of destiny, they spew forth the orders of fate or they lament and laud, remember and cherish.

Still other muscles move as Destiny draws her lines of life and death, as with feet spread wide in a stance of planted power, she sounds out the inexorable minutes of time. Ignacio girds himself for his duty and marches toward his doom. Woman racks her body, contorting it with anguish, bending it in useless supplication, rushing along the arc of action toward madness, spreading forth her arms and opening herself to receive and then release the spirit of her beloved.

And, at last, the muscles of Ignacio stir again, freed by Woman, free to move eternally through the memories of a life in which a strong body was the master in contest, the sharer in love, the representative of beauty and grandeur and courage.

Here in *Lament for Ignacio Sanchez Mejias* is a metaphor in muscles, an allegory in drama, for it is an aspect of man's existence, a comment upon his fate. Ignacio is a bullfighter, but his experience is universal; Ignacio is Spanish, but the portrait is painted with dyes from American roots.

The *Lament for Ignacio* is danced by three and none of these three is Doris Humphrey, yet she is there, for behind each step, each pattern, each idea, each surge of passion, each aperture opening upon vision, is the genius of one who traveled the arc of dance fearlessly and found greatness.

10

Weidman—Holm—Tamiris

The curtains, made of sheets, were drawn back, the parlor became a stage and the young boy commenced to dance. "There is someone dancing behind you, Charles," said the spiritualist friend of the boy's mother, and Charles, partly to assure himself of the friendly nature of the unseen spirit, murmured to himself, "It's probably Aunt Jessie doing her high kicks and stuff."

In one way or another, fancy-dancing, gay Aunt Jessie has been dancing with Charles Weidman ever since. If her specter is not actually present, her effervescent spirit makes itself felt in those of his dances which are carefree, boisterous and slightly zany.

Years later, a grown-up Charles Weidman brought Aunt Jessie to life in a distinguished solo work, *On My Mother's Side*. As Weidman visualized her, she fluttered and skipped coquettishly, danced prettily and appeared to be having the time of her life in her reincarnation. But if the heritage of Aunt Jessie bequeathed a sense of levity to her nephew, other forebears touched him with different gifts. And, as *On My Mother's Side* unfolded, a genetic pattern was established and brought to immediate life through the movements of dance.

A great-grandfather tilled the soil with loving hands, walking upon it with firm tread, bending toward it, seeming to breathe of it. The grandmother went about her labors of sweeping and sewing, of tracing her ritual of homely tasks; a hand brushed across the eyes, the shadows deepened and blindness came; there was a fleeting shudder of shock and then, tentatively at first and later with sweet assurance, the hands resumed their tasks, the body its duties, as the blind grandmother continued her needed ritual with the eyes of memory.

Next came the grandfather, who moved unbuffeted through a life design which he pursued as it came to him, and another grandfather, who frantically built homes of wood, built his life upon destructible material, saw his homes burn and hanged himself. In the actions of these forebears one found serenity and vigor, tragedy and fun, dedication and irresponsibility, love of the God-made and passion for the man-made, and in the newest path of this family pattern was the figure of Sonny, who partook of not one but of all these characteristics, who directed them and harnessed them to serve a new life program, the program of dance.

With the exception of the almost legendary Aunt Jessie, there was no one in Charles Weidman's family who could have been suspected of bequeathing to him a love of theater, let alone a talent for dance. Born in Lincoln, Nebraska, of American pioneer stock, the young Charles early developed a passion for dance. First, it was ballroom dancing—the only kind of dancing he knew—which consumed his energies.

Next, he hopped around as a grasshopper in a Nebraska pageant and became enthralled with the toe-traveling actions of a girl who appeared in the same pageant. Finally, he saw the Denishawn Dancers on tour, and their performance settled everything for him. He determined to become a dancer.

At first he danced in the family parlor, with the ghost of Aunt Jessie behind him, but soon he outgrew the parlor and delighted, amused, bewildered or horrified an audience at his school with a program of homemade, self-taught dances which included Russian, Aztec, Greek, Spanish, Egyptian, East Indian, Javanese and American Indian themes.

Following some preliminary ballet studies with Eleanor Frampton in Lincoln, Charles, at the age of seventeen, set out for California and Denishawn. Before long he became a member of the famed company (1920) and was sublimely happy dancing everything from a Toltec king to an American crapshooter. But as he developed as a dancer, the first pangs of discontent beset him. It occurred to the youthful Weidman that at Denishawn he was cast in either an exotic role or a character role, and, although these were just the sort of parts he had originally been seeking, he began to wonder, "What am I?" He wanted, of course, to become himself, and he felt that he could find himself not in variations of ethnologic dance forms but in dances which were distinctly American, as he understood the term.

For Weidman, the break with Denishawn led to greater difficulties than it did for either Graham or Humphrey. The two women set about their dance experiments with care, purpose and resolve. Weidman, on the other hand, was completely lost. He knew only the Denishawn way which he had abandoned, and, although he sensed what he wanted to do, he had not the faintest idea what method to pursue to reach his new goal. "I just went into the studio and couldn't move," he states.

He continued to be unable to move over a period long enough to terrify him, and, in desperation, decided to go to Ronny Johansson—a young artist of the German modern-dance school whom Shawn had brought to Denishawn to teach—for training and guidance. At this point, however, Humphrey put her foot down, convinced Weidman that he should not flee from his newly found freedom even to go to one he respected and admired, and urged him to "work it out yourself." With fresh determination, he returned to the studio and slowly began to discover his own way of dancing.

In the years that followed, Weidman created *Marionette Theater, The Happy Hypocrite, Candide* and, in the early 1930's, brought his comic skill to Broadway as choreographer, sometimes in association with Humphrey and sometimes on his own, for such shows as *Americana, As Thousands Cheer* and *Life Begins at 8:40.*

But Broadway, if it supplied money, did not answer a need. "I gave up good offers," he says, "to do what I felt compelled to do, to assume the obligations of a dance pioneer, to dance those ideas which I believed must be danced." And as he left Broadway, he entered upon years of hardship and economic insecurity. But they were to be years of rich creation.

One of his first compositions following the Broadway period was *Kinetic Pantomime,* a riotous dance which was as significant as it was fun. Here, in a brief solo, was crystallized pure dance humor, kinetic humor. Previously, Weidman had succeeded in mating pantomime with dance, gestural humor with pure movement, but *Kinetic Pantomime* was the perfect symbol of a new form and of Weidman's highly personal genius. The work owed nothing to stock pantomime, to representational movements used as replacements for words. The giggles were in the muscles, which made not literal jokes but, rather, muscle sense and nonsense.

His years of association with Doris Humphrey brought forth such distinguished works as *Opus 51, Quest, Atavisms, Flickers, On My Mother's Side, And Daddy Was a Fireman, David and Goliath, A House Divided* and episodes in two of Humphrey's masterworks, *Theater Piece* and *New Dance.* The titles alone provide clues to the range of material at his command: delicate portraits of Weidman's ancestors, the brutal ceremony of lynching, the slapstick activities of a floorwalker and his bargain-searching females, the plea of Lincoln for equality and unity.

With Opus 51, he expanded the material of *Kinetic Pantomime* into a full-scale ballet, proving that the principle of purely motor humor could apply to others than himself and could be formalized into group patterns. With *Quest,* he turned his humor and his venom on the difficulties which beset the artist in the persons of addlepated patronesses, blind critics and the like.

Humor was used to strike at injustice in *Quest,* but in *Lynch Town* (from his *Atavisms* suite) grim horror was the keynote. In this work the audience witnessed not only the injustice with which a minority group of our population has been treated but also the primitive blood lust, the sadism which supposedly civilized persons reveal when a scapegoat for their bigoted savagery is found.

Lynch Town strikes home, it strikes the very being of the American, for the trembling evil of the lynchers themselves and the evil of the lookers-on who share vicariously in the horrible thrill seem to vibrate across the footlights and attack the complacency of those who sit in the safety of the theater. The dancers move with racing frenzy, halting to look at death with lust and, perhaps, with fear. A figure stretches forward to get a better view of murder, and horror stretches along the invisible waves of art communication to remind the beholder that the battle for "the land of the free and the home of the brave" is not yet won.

Two of Weidman's most engaging creations are *Flickers* and *Fables for Our Time.* The former, as the title indicates, treats of the early movies, its forms, themes and scuttling characters, in four episodes (or reels) : "Hearts Aflame," in which the hero saves the heroine from a mortgage foreclosure and the advances of the villain; "Wages of Sin," featuring a Theda Bara–style vamp who writhes her way into a married man's heart, breaks up his home and makes him a corpse; "Flowers of the Desert," with one like Valentino setting feminine hearts aflutter; and a Western occupied with cowboys and Indians.

In *Fables for Our Time,* based upon the Thurber stories, Weidman combines the use of speech (as he has in many other creations) with dance action. In one of the fables, while the narrator is describing, in Thurber's own words, the female chipmunk who industriously and determinedly stores up nuts against the day when they will be needed and the male chipmunk who is primarily concerned with the decorative value of nuts, Weidman extends the Thurber images into action. As the male chipmunk, he delightedly places oversize acorns between his fingers as if they were giant rings, or plants them between his toes and launches into a happy fandango, or, with winning rudeness, contemplates the aesthetic value of the acorns as he places them against the ample posterior of the female.

Fables and *Flickers* are fun, light in spirit, adroitly choreographed and understandable to anyone. If Weidman had been content to work exclusively as a comic, Broadway would have been happy to have him and he would have been content with Broadway. But the man who could clown also had some serious things to say in dance, and Broadway shows offered but rare opportunities to a choreographer who felt the necessity of dancing about injustice, of drawing a portrait of Lincoln in dance, of experimenting with new forms.

As he grew older, he turned more and more to teaching, not only in New York studios but as a highly successful "itinerant" teacher in studios and especially in colleges from coast to coast. Still, by the 1970's he was continuing to present dance programs, including new choreographies, in his tiny studio-theater in New York.

The gay spirit of Aunt Jessie is always around Charles Weidman, but the instincts and needs of the pioneer have colored his dancing, teaching and choreography for more than four decades, defining him as one of the major figures in America's modern dance: first a rebel, then a reformer, always a builder.

"I have come to you because I want to learn how to talk with my back," said the great Russian ballerina to the little

German-American dancer. Other dancers—ballet, modern, musical comedy—have come to Hanya Holm for the same and for different reasons but all bearing the conviction that Hanya Holm could make them better dancers. In a sense, this is a strange conviction, for Holm has been the least active performance-wise of all the leaders of modern dance.

Some are too young to have remembered her masterpiece, *Trend,* and many, undoubtedly, missed seeing her rare subsequent performances in New York; few professionals, one supposes, have seen her annual summertime dance productions at Colorado College; yet the young student seems to know that Hanya Holm can build dancers. It is possible that the very infrequency of her own performing—although she has been an active choreographer for Broadway shows—provides the student with the assurance that she will not stamp him with the personal idiosyncrasies of her own way of dance, that she will not turn him into a miniature Holm, but that she will discover and nurture the dance that is within him.

As for an inner dance, Holm has always possessed it. Even as a child in Worms on the Rhine in Germany, her subconscious love of movement found release at a convent school where a dancing master trained the girls in the social graces. She learned the waltz step and schottische, but she also became fascinated with the words the teacher spoke: "moving feet," "carriage," "uprightness"—words she never forgot.

When she was only eight, Jaques Dalcroze presented a music pantomime for the children, using the body to perform his songs, and little Hanya found "moving feet," "carriage" and "uprightness" again.

Even if she had consciously known that she wanted to

become a dancer, Hanya would have found difficulties, for ballet in Germany was at a low level, considered inferior to the other arts and frowned upon by nice people as a career for a nice girl. Her apparent musical skill was, however, recognized by her family, and piano studies were approved. But her music teacher, evidently an observant gentleman, told his student that she was on the wrong track. "You tend to move," he said, and suggested that she pursue her studies at the new Dalcroze school at Frankfurt-am-Main, where she would be able to investigate the physical approach to music.

Toward the end of World War I, she moved to Dresden to continue her lessons at the Dalcroze school in that city and ultimately passed her examinations for a Dalcroze proficiency certificate. But with her graduation and the end of the war a decision was inevitable, although she was still torn between dance and music. With the help of the drama of the times, the tragedies and frustrations and heightened passions which affected her fellow countrymen, dance won, for she felt that the drama of dance, the employment of her entire body were needed in the life before her.

If Holm took her first step toward nonconformity by flying in the face of middle-class convention and selecting dance as her chosen work, her second step, never to be re-traced, led her into the ranks of those nonconformists who gave birth to a new dance.

In spite of her tininess, grace and winsome beauty, ballet was not for her. There were opportunities and invitations, but the easy way to dance success, the path of convention, did not appeal to her. Because the stress of the times had led her to a dance decision in the first place, she went, inevitably, to the great dance revolutionary of Germany, Mary Wigman.

Holm shared with Wigman the wonders and the trials of experimentation. They traveled alone in the European dance world, testing all routes to dance fulfillment, predicating their work upon trial and error, digging frantically for undiscovered dance ores. At times they produced dance fragments of utter awkwardness; again they produced dance fragments of stirring strength.

Their fellow citizens looked upon them with mistrust, regarded them through eyes accustomed to and, perhaps, content with a moribund ballet form. They (the public) mistook convention for beauty, and Wigman, along with Holm and other art rebels, tried desperately to swim against the stream of contaminated convention. They were laughed at, sneered at and continued to face abuses, but they had the courage and strength to battle for the defeat of sugary prettiness and for the triumph of beauty, of inner illumination.

As the 1920's drew to a close, Wigman's success drew near. Holm was placed in charge as head teacher of the Wigman school, appeared as a principal dancer in the concert group and aided Wigman in the production of *Totenmal*, the antiwar dance work presented at the Dance Congress in Munich in 1930. Shortly thereafter, Wigman and her company came to America and, after their engagements, returned home, leaving Hanya Holm behind in New York as head of a new branch of the Wigman school.

Holm had not been here very long when she realized that although the Wigman system had much to offer Americans, it would have to be adapted to the needs and characteristics of a new land. Here was a land not spent by war, not marked by tragedy, but a land with vigorous people, assured, lively, filled with gusto and humor. The principles and some of the forms of the Wigman dance would apply to Americans, but the themes, the national characteristics, of the Wigman art would not. Holm severed all connections with the mother institution and set about the business of becoming an American citizen and an American dancer.

For six years after her arrival in America, Hanya Holm did not perform. She used those years to study her new home and its people, to absorb its flavors, to experience the force of its customs and to adapt her concept of dance to the needs of the dance students of America. When finally, in 1937, she produced her first major dance work, *Trend*, it was an American one and a great one. Meanwhile, she had become a part of the modern American dance effort, and, because she was equipped with a definite concept of dance and supported by a highly developed technique, she also became, in spite of her inactivity in the theater, a dance power.

In teaching her students, Holm stresses the fact that the impulse to dance action may be physical, emotional or mental, but that each stimulus possesses a center from which it radiates. There are movements, of course, which are peripheral as well as central, movements which seem to channel into the body as well as those which extend from it, movements which are born of contracting muscles as well as movements which come from muscular release. Yet Holm points out that when the body is traveling forward and appears to be mainly frontal, the back of the body is also present and also moving for the simple reason that a center continues to exist.

3) It is a concept, this centrality of the body, which makes possible full-bodied action, which gives action a starting point, which provides a dynamo core to dance and which enables the dancer to maintain balance in even the most gravity-provoking situation. The Russian ballerina who came to Holm because she wanted to "learn how to talk with my back" could not have found a better answer to her problem than the "centrality" of Holm.

The dancer stands on her toes, the "uprightness" of her baby lessons remembered; verticality is established. In this position, in the position which represents man's evolutionary and revolutionary departure from animal existence, the center of the body is most clearly recognized, a plumb line from head to toe.

But the dancer commences to move, she steps forth, she swings her body into a spiraling turn, she leans forward, suspending her body not over her feet but over space. Yet wherever she moves she is aware of the center of her body, the center of balance, the center of action. Motions spring forth not chaotically but like the spokes of a wheel which find a permanent source and center in the hub.

The dancer is doing more than maintaining balance, displaying ordered movement, revealing control of a center. Her steps are easy and simple, but the spiral turn is flooded with greater intensity and the suspension is marked by a flash of arrested action. Perhaps, as she moves along, she begins to tread more heavily, her body pushing with greater eagerness toward its goal. An arm may move in a gentle arc and later, describing the same path, in an arc of strength. The dancer, in order to achieve certain dramatic effects, is simply loading her movements with the desired intensity, an intensity which is "driven" out of the body rather than "applied" to it in artificial fashion.

Here is an intensity which springs from the center of being, that hub of the physical, emotional or mental stimulus. With this use of intensity, with the opening and closing of the taps of energy, the dancer is able to give her actions variety of shading comparable to that of the musician with his instrument or with his voice, comparable to the painter with his hues of varying density, comparable to the architect with his beams, his boards, his laths and his lattices.

The dancer not only maintains her "center" and "loads" her movements with varying degrees of intensity, but she also "travels" through space. Space is ahead of her, behind her, to her sides, above and below her. She investigates, she explores the drama of space, and she marks that space with formal patterns as surely as the painter patterns the canvas before him, but, more than that, her travel through space reveals her purpose.

And what is the purpose of these principles, which, at first glance, seem to be highly technical, remote from the excitement of theater? The purpose of the Holm dance is to "convey idea through form," through the form of a constantly centered body, through the form of dynamic stress, through the form created by a purposeful body moving through space.

There is drama even in the cold technical studies which the students do at a Holm class. Watching them, one sees, of course, the fundamental stretchings and strengthenings of the body, but soon one becomes aware of the body forces struggling against the pull of gravity, the weight of gravity, and there are seeds of drama in this very elemental but endless conflict. The struggle itself leads the students to a discovery of that powerful center, the inner man, the nucleus of being from which the forces which are to repel the magnetic weight of gravity must emanate.

As the students cross the floor with a stride, a dipping turn, a leap, a lunge toward the ground, a thrust to a moment of vertical suspension, they constantly shift those forces which can defeat gravity, deploying them to new body locations, using them strategically but maintaining a supply line of energy from that center of being which generates forces and reinforcements. Inevitably, the center moves as the dancers move along spatial distances to new spatial centers, new arenas of action, and each purposeful action calls for dynamic coloring.

This is classwork, but it is also dance. It is a dance which, because of its full-bodiedness, its disclosure of the inner man, "hits you in the solar plexus and in the brain," says Holm, whereas the ofttimes frontal style of the strictly classical ballet may "hit you only in the eyes."

With such training, the Holm students do not become regimented, for they are taught principles which Holm feels can govern whatever style of dance they may prefer: ballet, modern, tap, jazz or personal ways of theatrical expression. If her students are taught to create form, they are also taught how to fill form with life and purpose so that if a finished dance is given to them, they can realize, with conviction, its potentialities. It is a technique which is neither a routine nor a vocabulary but a means to an end, a way of reaching full-ness in art expression.

Although Hanya Holm, as a modern-dance leader, has established herself as one of the great teachers, her theatrical career cannot be overlooked. With her company, active in the late 1930's and early 1940's, she produced not only the monumental *Trend*, but also *Tragic Exodus*, based on the plight of the Nazi-persecuted Jews; *Dance of Introduction*, a jubilant dance of greeting; *Metropolitan Daily* and other works, serious and light.

Dance of Work and Play, Orestes and the Furies, What So Proudly We Hail, What Dreams May Come, Ozark Suite, Windows and *Walt Whitman Suite* account for still further productions in a repertory created either for her own company or for her semiprofessional summertime group at Colorado College.

Holm choreography familiar to the largest public is not that created for her concert group or for her festival units but, rather, for Broadway shows. In *Ballet Ballads*, which engaged the services of three choreographers, one for each of its three episodes, Holm choreographed *The Eccentricities of Davy Crockett* and walked off with top honors. With *Kiss Me, Kate*, she was associated with a smash Broadway hit and, as choreographer, had an opportunity to apply her dance principles to an elaborate show involving the allied arts.

In *Kate* she augmented the values of songs with the expressional powers of dance, she established group characteristics through dance, she did set routines, and she proved that her dance could serve as a diversion, a dramatic high spot, a coloring, a short cut to exposition, a discipline, a form of human eloquence.

Her most spectacular Broadway success was, of course, *My Fair Lady*, which established new box-office records both in New York City and in countries around the world. Other shows, movies, opera, television, dance dramas and continuing, though limited, teaching schedules have kept her constantly on the American dance scene.

"I guess I'm in the wrong place," said the fifteen-year-old girl. All about her were young ladies in neat ballet costumes and toe slippers, and there she was, barelegged, barefooted and dressed in gymnasium-like practice clothes. But the lady in charge told her to go ahead and dance. The long, strong legs struck out in easy strides or bore her upward in joyous leaps, the body bent and dipped with sturdy grace and the air seemed freshened by the physical exuberance of healthy youth.

The lady in charge approved, and Helen Tamiris, later to become one of the foremost nonconformists of dance, was engaged for her first job as a ballet dancer with the Metropolitan Opera Ballet. Apparently, even the Metropolitan's prima ballerina, Rosina Galli, had recognized a native skill in the girl, a talent worthy of being fostered and certainly worth leading into balletic channels.

It must have been clear even then that the energetic redhead could not stop with ballet. Everything about her being, everything about her background made a ballet career, no matter how successful, impossible. She had come from the streets of New York, was trained on those streets, and because she both loved and hated those streets it was a foregone conclusion, unknown to her at the time, that she would one day find it necessary to dance about them and to dance about the people who traveled other streets, avenues, lanes and pathways of her land.

As Helen Becker, Tamiris was born of Russian Jewish parents in New York's Lower East Side and "with one leg in the gutter," as she herself averred. Perhaps, due to the remembered or quoted expressions of her parents, she felt the sinister qualities of the neighborhood, the gloom of a nearby prison, and sensed that, although she was born in a free land, the heritage of her parents permitted the shadow of a ghetto to cloud, upon occasion, her spirit. But in spite of poverty, inherited tragedy, of gloomy surroundings and of a family life complicated, through the early years, by two stepmothers, Helen liked to dance and danced in the only available places, the streets.

One of her brothers found her dancing merrily along the sidewalks and urged their father to give her dancing lessons. At eight, then, she began her dance study at the Henry Street Settlement under the guidance of Irene Lewisohn, who, like St. Denis, had been guided by the principles of Delsarte.

Much to her father's dismay, Helen's basic urge to dance had by no means been exhausted by the ensuing years of study with Irene Lewisohn. To the contrary, not only was the urge to dance stronger, but the will to dance was adamant. Mr. Becker, though a poor man, wanted his only daughter to go to college and somehow he would have arranged for this continuation of her education. Helen would have none of it and, equipped with her strong limbs, her Lewisohn discipline and determination, turned up for the Metropolitan auditions and won a contract which promised her three months of free ballet lessons and twelve dollars a week (plus three lessons a week) thereafter.

After four years of dancing Italian ballet at the Metropolitan, and a summer season as second ballerina with an opera company in South America, Helen Becker determined to make a change. She had selected a new name for herself, Tamiris, taken from the final line of a poem concerning a Persian queen: "Thou art Tamiris, the ruthless queen who banishes all obstacles." Willing, at least, to attack all obstacles, and feeling reasonably certain that she could, like her Persian queen, vanquish them, she left behind her an established position with the Metropolitan and set forth for new adventures.

For a time, under the tutelage of Michel Fokine, she was content with the freer, more energetic style of Russian ballet, with the exuberant character dances he taught her and with a performing season in the ballet prelude he created for *Casanova*. But, still restless, she moved on to a Duncan studio, where she felt that she would find opportunities to dance as she wanted to dance. Isadora had been the great liberator, the first to free the dancer from the bonds of accepted technique, but Tamiris soon discovered that the Duncan school she was attending had, as far as Tamiris was concerned, remembered something of method but had forgotten or foresworn the testament of freedom.

Next, as a specialty dancer, she did a stint in Chicago night clubs and then went into the fourth *Music Box Revue* to perform a Chinese dance and to enact the Red Queen in an "Alice in Wonderland" skit. Then, with sufficient escape money saved from her commercial ventures, she jumped into the creation of her first concert program.

In preparing this first program, Tamiris discovered the reason for her silent revolution. Her desire to be an American dancer led her to the creation of an American program in which she wanted to capture the movement idioms of the American Negro, the prizefighter, the inhabitant of a jazz era and others who lived in the America of the 1920's. It was plain that the vocabularies of the Italian ballet, the Russian ballet, the Spanish dance and the Duncan system could not possibly give valid substance to such themes. A new vocabulary had to be created in order to create the dances themselves.

She discovered almost immediately, however, that not even she could create a permanent technique, that her fundamental principles of movement could never become crystallized into a set vocabulary. Never could she foist established movement patterns upon selected content; rather, she would draw, extract movement from whatever content her theme proposed.

With her approach to American dance clear in her mind, Tamiris composed her program of *Dance Moods* and presented it at New York's Little Theater, October 9, 1927. The debut was eminently successful, at least as successful as any modern-dance program could have been in those days.

The following year, the Mozarteum Society invited her to dance at Salzburg, and her performances there and in Paris

and Berlin were enthusiastically received. Her jazz compositions, spirituals and athletic studies seemed genuinely American to her European audiences, and her experiments with
nude dancing (which did not come into Broadway acceptance until forty years later) were accepted as serious and
artistic tests. In spite of her success in Europe and her
inevitable contacts with the powerful and surging Central
European school of modern dance, she returned to America
still "rampantly of the New World," as one writer remarked.

For Tamiris, 1929 was a year of importance. The major
critics commenced to probe for the secret of her dance
qualities: one found her "an emotional dancer, a stylist and a
dynamo of energy and blunt force, fearless, direct and pro-
pulsive," while another said of her Negro spirituals, "not
translation but illumination."

Her 1929 program carried more than a hint of her concern
with the social problems of the day, for *Revolutionary March*
and *Dance of the City,* with its disclosure of repression,
heralded an era of social comment in modern dance. Violent
about being an American dancer, violent in her nonconformity, she was equally violent in her revelation of social and
economic ills, real or fancied, major or minor. The same
tempestuous energy which flooded nonobjective dances with
fire, power and stormy beauty filled her dances of social
significance with indignation, conviction and anger, and if
they were not all worthy of her inherent skill, they were
genuinely alive.

In the same year, with defiance in her eye and fists
clenched, she formed her first dance group and along with it

issued a statement in which she blasted the ballet and condemned any group which felt that it could create American dance simply by using American dancers while continuing to employ movement techniques imported from Europe or the Orient.

Later that year, she helped found the Dance Repertory Theater, established for American dancers and featuring the works of Martha Graham, Doris Humphrey, Charles Weidman and, of course, Tamiris herself. For two seasons—1930 and 1931—the organization endured, playing to small but ardent audiences, and with its termination Tamiris concentrated upon building her own company's repertory and in creating works for the Federal Theater Project of the Works Progress Administration, in which she was an active and dominant figure.

As her attitude toward dance grew in scope and as her convictions were deepened by choreographic experimentations, she began to lay stress more than ever upon dances of social comment. In the 1930's she created *Cycle of Unrest,* composed of "Protest," "Camaraderie," "Conflict," "The Individual and the Masses"; *Momentum,* made up of "Unemployed," "SH! SH!," "Legion," "Nightriders," "Diversion," "Disclosure"; *How Long Brethren,* one of her most successful works, divided into "Pickin' Off de Cotton," "Upon de Mountain," "Scottsboro," "Let's Go to de Buryin'" and "How Long Brethren"; *Adelante,* a protest against the cruelties of the Spanish Civil War.

None of these dances of protest were unqualified successes in the minds of many of the critics, for although sections and even whole episodes were cited for their excellences, there was a feeling that the themes were not always realized in terms of clear and concise choreography.

Not all, however, was protest. During the same decade she created her *Walt Whitman Suite,* which used such poems as "Salut au Monde," "I Sing the Body Electric," "Halcyon Days" and "Song of the Road." These were highly successful, for the lusty Whitman and the lusty Tamiris had much in common. With these poetic springboards, she was able to propel herself into an affirmative America and not a protesting one, flooding the stage with an abundance of energy, gusto and free beauty such as Whitman would have relished.

With the end of the Federal Theater Project and the close of the 1930's, modern dance reached a financial ebb. The tours of the middle thirties were no more, and because of the ever-increasing expense of Broadway engagements, studio performances became the rule. Tamiris also turned to studio outlets for her creations, and in her little headquarters in downtown New York she produced one of her most impressive, jubilant and all-round attractive works, *Liberty Song.* Her period of choreographic protest was over and she was again affirmative in spirit.

Liberty Song was as richly American as any dance could be, for it was American in theme, in history, in tradition, in costuming, in music, in accompanying text, in spirit and, of course, in the dance technique employed in its production. Tamiris had always fought to "break down the arbitrary use of the spoken word for the communication of an idea." With *Liberty Song* she was prepared to go still further, to convince the theater that it need not employ dance only as a medium of communication but that it should use "the activity of

movement" in conjunction with "all forms of expression."
Liberty Song was obviously a dance and a great one, but for
Tamiris it signified a drive toward a new kind of theater.

Based upon the songs of the American Revolution—"What
a Court Hath Old England," "My Days Have Been So
Wondrous Free," "Bunker Hill," "Ode to the Fourth of
July"—*Liberty Song* was alive with humor and romance,
affirmation and power. Because of its songs and its staging, it
evoked the past, but because of the immediacy of dance, it
brought the elements of dance down to the present.

Bunker Hill became more than a patriotic milestone when
danced, for the surge and strength of those men who had
fought at Bunker Hill again infused the bodies of Americans,
contemporary Americans, and reminded them and the beholder that the spirit of Bunker Hill must never die. The
satire, sturdy and pungent but not bitter, in "What a Court
Hath Old England" reminded us of the opinions of our forebears but prodded us to be ever alert for evidences of moral
decay. Further, it demonstrated the rough and fearless
American humor which helped to free the colonists and
which has continued to aid in keeping us free in thought and
deed.

On the personal plane was the warm romance of "My Days
Have Been So Wondrous Free." Here was a lass of the
Revolution bidding farewell to her lover as he sailed away.
There were warmth and openness in her affection, femininity
in her actions, but a robust strength in her stance and pride
in the tilt of her head. As one watched them together, the
past seemed to merge with the present in the timeless cherish-
ing of freedom, of wondrous freedom.

With the studio presentation of *Liberty Song* in 1941, Tamiris was ready to embark upon a new area based upon her concept of total theater. Now was the time to go back to Broadway, not as a specialty dancer but as a choreographer prepared to use movement and other modes of artistic expression for the communication of ideas. Musical comedies had changed since the 1920's and there were now opportunities for a choreographer such as Helen (she introduced her first name at this time) Tamiris.

Tamiris returned to Broadway not for money alone, not for a financial security she had earned through years of independent service to dance progress, but because she knew that her way of dance could be used effectively in the new type of musical which was heading in the direction of what has been described as "the lyric theater."

In her choreography for Broadway, Tamiris did not cheapen her art. She did not face the problem of "deintellectualizing" her approach to dance, for she had always been forthright and simple, her themes had been about ordinary people and much of her work had depended for its effect upon the uninhibited power and natural beauty of her movement. She simply applied these principles to the tasks at hand, and although she might not have, of her own accord, elected to do an American Indian ballet *(Annie Get Your Gun)* or character movement treating with persons moving in Boss Tweed's circle of friends *(Up in Central Park)*, she knew that the solid craft of her dance could do the jobs and do them well.

In almost every one of her Broadway shows, she worked valiantly and successfully to weave dancing into the very fabric of the show itself so that it was difficult to tell where acting ended and dancing began, where choreography ceased and general staging returned. Even in *Annie Get Your Gun* Tamiris kept the Indian ballet from being an isolated production number by working the nondancing star of the show, Ethel Merman, into the action, thus linking dance with drama and song through one individual and through the splicing of acting and action.

Other shows included *Showboat, Inside U.S.A., Fanny, Plain and Fancy, Touch and Go.* In 1960, with her dancer-husband Daniel Nagrin, she established a new concert group, the Tamiris-Nagrin Dance Company. She choreographed new pieces for this unit, but she also choreographed or re-staged older works for the Juilliard Dance Theatre, for the High School of the Performing Arts, for dance centers in Colorado, Utah, Maine and elsewhere. Her vitality as a choreographer, coach, teacher and personality remained with her until her untimely death in 1966.

To Tamiris, dancing was a part of living, and through her own dancing and choreography she attempted to give the American public as sturdy a commodity as the master shoe-maker gives the public through his shoes. One may be an intangible commodity and the other tangible, but both are real and both are of use to all Americans.

If the day ever comes, and it must, when the American public looks upon dance and the artist-dancer as essential not only to his culture but to his very life, one may be sure that Tamiris will be there in spirit.

Part III

The Rich Present

11

The Fruits of Modern Dance

For young artists to follow in the footsteps of titans is not a particularly happy lot. Thus it was with a new generation of modern dancers, with those who came after Graham, Humphrey and their fellow pioneers and who were forced not only to follow but also to attempt to rival the continuing creativeness and, in some instances, the performing magnitude of the masters.

The titans had made the break with the past, evolved new principles, battled convention, won the rebellion. What was left to be done? Some of the young moderns were content to imitate their great teachers. Others, defiant, sought to escape influences, both good and bad, and to be different, at all costs, from anything or anybody. A few had the good sense to learn all they could from the titans, to be influenced but not intimidated and to pursue the modern-dance course most suitable to their basic talents, temperament and ideas.

Of all who immediately followed the titans, José Limón

was the most successful, both as dancer and choreographer. Indeed, he joined them as one of the major figures on the modern-dance scene. For although he did not belong to the generation of pioneers, he entered the new art area they opened up, and explored and exploited its resources with power, with vision, with originality.

As a leading dancer in the Humphrey-Weidman Company, Limón demonstrated his fundamental dance skill. He was big, he was strong and he moved with the dignity befitting a man. But it was not until he had seen service in the armed forces during World War II, matured as a man and as a performer and set out on his own that he began to achieve that artistry which was to make him the most distinguished male dancer in the modern field.

With Doris Humphrey as his artistic director and co-choreographer for his company, Limón built a performing repertory surpassed in box-office appeal and prestige only by that of Martha Graham.

Limón's appeal as a dancer lay not only in his technical skill (he is now retired as a dancer), but also in his bearing, in his coloring of dance movement. His Mexican Indian heritage shows in his finely sculptured face, and the enormous dignity of the Indian was always present in his dance movements. The warmth he feels for mankind, the concern he bears for the welfare of his fellow men were also present in his dancing, along with intense passion and a command of the heroic.

Of his own choreographies, the best known and the most popular is *The Moor's Pavane,* a dance treatment of the story of Othello. To convey the drama of this tale, he has, of course, used the technique of modern dance, but he has cast it, as the title suggests, into court dance forms. The four figures—Othello, Desdemona, Iago, Emilia—move with the greatest of elegance through these formal dance patterns, patterns which are harshly broken, interrupted by primitive bursts of villainy, deceit, hate, vengeance and, finally, murder.

With splendid power, surface behavior and inner compulsions are interrelated in *The Moor's Pavane* in the finest tradition of modern-dance principles, in the highest tradition of the theater. As the sometimes sweet, sometimes impassioned music of Purcell guides the form of the dance or spurs the revelation of emotion, the four characters speed toward their doom. *The Moor's Pavane* has been done as an art movie, and, in 1969, as a dance classic, was added to the repertory of the American Ballet Theatre, thus demonstrating the increasing interdependence of ballet and modern dance.

In *La Malinche* Limón turned to his native Mexico for dance inspiration. Here there are three figures and they first come upon the stage as if they were village performers prepared, at festival time, to retell a story familiar to all their neighbors. The girl becomes Malinche, the Indian maiden who betrayed her people to the white invader; the fair-haired man enacts the part of the conquistador and El Indio was originally danced by Limón.

As this story in dance unfolds, we watch Malinche submit willingly to the conqueror, embrace him and his new religion and give him a rose, a symbol of Mexico. As El Indio is crushed, Malinche dons the heavy garments of another culture, attempts to escape from her own heritage, but she, too, now that she is no longer needed, is spurned by the invader she helped.

Contrite, Malinche repents, but it is too late and her own people, represented by the figure of El Indio, disown her. Then El Indio rises from defeat and attempts to win back all he has lost. In his battle against the conqueror, he hears footsteps behind him and finds it is the spirit of the repentant Malinche there to guide him, to encourage him, to redeem herself. Together they fight, together they win, and, at the end of the story, Malinche recovers the rose and with a simple, heartfelt gesture returns it to El Indio. The tale, oft-told, is done; the dancers bow and leave.

Here, in *La Malinche,* is a perfect example of the way that modern dance can thrive and grow. Limón, a devoted but not enslaved disciple of Humphrey and Weidman, took their principles of movement and from them evolved actions and gestures which would serve a theme remote from the experiences of either Humphrey or Weidman but close to Limón himself. He had created a modern-dance theater piece, but, more than that, he had created a work which revealed his own individual artistry.

But Mexican themes actually were represented less frequently in the Limón repertory than themes derived from other sources. He has, for example, choreographed non-narrative dances to music of Bach, Vivaldi and contemporary composers, and he has turned to religious settings for his *The Visitation,* an unusual, humble, extremely simple and very human view of the Annunciation, and for *The Traitor,* a work for an all-male company built around the figure of

Judas and his betrayal of Christ. This is also in the repertory of the American Ballet Theatre.

With the immeasurably valuable assistance of Humphrey, as adviser and contributing choreographer, and with such highly polished dancers in his company as Pauline Koner, an experienced choreographer and a brilliant dance soloist in her own right; Lucas Hoving, also an independent choreographer and a skillful dramatic dancer; José Limón achieved not only national but also international prominence. In the 1960's Koner, Hoving and other senior dancers went their separate ways, with the Limón company continuing with a new—the third—generation of modern dancers.

Valerie Bettis, whose major modern-dance heritage stems from Hanya Holm, achieved such recognition as an actress, as a star dancer in musical comedies and as a choreographer for both Broadway and Hollywood that there was an unfortunate tendency to overlook her attainments in the theater of modern dance. A vivid performer with a vitality akin to that of Tamiris but with a dramatic intensity all her own, Bettis used her dance gifts in a variety of roles. She was earthy, sexy and an expert satirist, and these qualities were present not only in her concert pieces but also in her work for the commercial theater.

One of her most distinguished choreographic achievements is *As I Lay Dying,* based upon the William Faulkner story. In it, she combines speech with dance to make a powerful dance drama of a woman's deathbed review of a life filled with tragedy, weariness and a single illicit love affair which bore the sweet fruit of a beloved son. With movies and the Broadway theater days behind her, Bettis not only staged her successful dances and created new dances for companies in various communities, but she also founded a workshop in which drama and dance, interrelated, were the chief subjects of experiments by a variety of choreographers and directors. Bettis herself occasionally choreographs for her Dancers Studio, but is chiefly concerned with supervising the creative programs involving dancers, choreographers, directors, composers and their colleagues.

In pursuits, John Butler has been like Bettis in that a good many of his efforts were concerned with the commercial theater and TV. Luckily, Butler has been associated with several of the more adventuresome television programs and has been able, consequently, to do more than make up steps to go with popular songs. Indeed, several of his most serious and avant-garde concert pieces have been adapted for television, and new works on the same level have been created especially for the medium.

As a dance descendant of Martha Graham, he turns, quite naturally, to dance ideas which strive to reveal the inner man, his ecstasies and his torments. Employing a choreographic style which is entirely his own (Graham principles are present, but there are no borrowed Graham movements), he has created an incredible array of arresting dance works for both modern dance companies and for ballet—in one twelve-month period, he created eight new works and restaged two older ones—for dance troupes in many states and foreign lands. These include the Royal Winnipeg Ballet, the Pennsylvania Ballet, the Boston Ballet, the Repertory Dance Theatre of Utah, the Harkness Ballet, the Netherlands Dance Theater, the New York City Opera, the Athens International

Festival, the Caramoor Festival, the Festival of Two Worlds (Spoleto, Italy), the Metropolitan Opera and more.

Many of his newest works have had their dramatic focus on man and his place in a violent world, ranging from *After Eden* (the agony of the expulsion) through the medieval poet *Villon,* to today's lost and tormented youth.

Modern dance is, of course, a nonconformist approach to the art, but there are, quite rightly, those who refuse to conform to the rather free patterns of form and behavior established by pioneering nonconformists. Among the most important of the nonconformists were Sybil Shearer, a onetime soloist in the Humphrey-Weidman Company, and Merce Cunningham, soloist with Martha Graham. Both have had long careers as avant-garde artists, yet they have retained almost exalted positions as the king and queen of the avant-garde—others come and go, but they stay on.

Miss Shearer, with an easy manner and a prodigious technique, is at her best as a soloist. She wears no makeup, has wispy hair and doesn't seem to care what she looks like, except that she does enjoy elaborate costumes as extensions of her dance fantasies. She is closely attuned to nature, and in her dances the viewer may become deeply affected by a gesture which suggests the caressing of a leaf or a reaching toward the sun or, in a gently turning body, the shimmer of moonlight. Her headquarters, studio and school, have long been in the Middle West, and since she dislikes cities and touring, her dance followers usually come to her. She is a dancer's dancer, and her audiences are always filled with other dancers who come to marvel at her imaginativeness, her simplicity. She might do an entire dance standing on one leg;

she has done a program of numbered but untitled dances; she has changed a program midway because the vibrations with an audience didn't seem quite right to her. Yet she can be a weaver of magic in dances with such wonderful titles as *Without Wings the Way Is Steep, Stamping Won't Dent the World, The Spark Is the Child of Flame* and *The Sunbeam Will Outlast Us All.*

As a dancer, Merce Cunningham also gives the impression of being closely allied to those forms of nature which lie outside the human body—although in his humorous moments one will see very human comments upon the frailties of man. But he does move with the speed, even the stealth, the alertness of an animal, and his leaps and jumps are not so much a display of physical prowess as they are catlike departures from the earth, resilient cleavages of space.

As a choreographer, he began his experiments before he left the Martha Graham Company in 1945, and already he was displaying a style totally unlike that of his teacher. One of his early solos was *Root of an Unfocus* (1944), which made clear that he was not interested in the sort of form and dramatic sequences that his seniors, and some of his contemporaries, were using in modern dance.

Cunningham has explored dance-by-chance methods, that is, not making designs and sequences deliberately but, instead, duplicating the patterns formed by Chinese sticks which have been tossed into the air and landed at random. He also frequently works on the theory that the music and the dance coexist in a given performance—the music, in other words, is not an accompaniment but an independent art expression going on at the same time that the dancers are moving. His long-time associate is the avant-garde composer, John Cage, who uses regular musical instruments, prepared pianos and all manner of electronic additions, including ear-splitting amplifications. Sometimes a sequence of a Cage score is governed by a stop watch, and the musicians may space out their notes to that time or play them all at once and sit back or rush them in at the end.

The dancers in the Cunningham company are among the most expert and brilliantly trained in the modern-dance field. He has enjoyed great success in Europe as well as in the United States and has been the recipient of grants from private foundations, federal and state governments. Of all America's avant-garde artists, he is certainly the most celebrated dancer and one who is a favorite with musicians and painters.

Another American avant-garde dance leader of international prominence is Paul Taylor, who formed his first company in 1954 when he was twenty-four years old. But unlike Cunningham, who, once he had become independent, remained an independent artist, Taylor danced leading roles for several seasons with Martha Graham and even appeared with the New York City Ballet as a guest artist while continuing his own experiments. Like Cunningham, he is a tall man, but he is stockier and he uses his long, muscular arms in great waving, swooping motions (Cunningham uses smaller gestures). For his choreographies, he has commissioned scores of modern composers, but he also has successfully used classical music while retaining a modern-dance approach. Indeed, his *Aureole,* to music of Handel, is in the repertory of the Royal Danish Ballet. But his creations are also set to music of the day's avant-garde composers, Cage among them, and even to the Laneville-Johnson Union Brass Band.

Taylor, too, has received support from state and federal funds, from independent foundations and has won awards for his work from Paris to Santiago to New York.

The fourth senior American avant-garde dance leader of world-wide stature is Alwin Nikolais, who stemmed from the Hanya Holm school. Shortly after he became director (1948) of the Henry Street Settlement Playhouse in New York City, Nikolais began his experiments with a new form of dance theater. Five years later, he was ready and his *Masks, Props and Mobiles* was produced. This was the first of a series of intensely theatrical avant-garde creations—*Kaleidoscope* and *Totem* were among many others—which were the fruits of his plan to have a theater in which "motion, sound, shape and color" were coequal ingredients. In this theater of his Nikolais, a trained musician as well as a dancer and an experienced puppeteer, not only choreographs, but composes his own scores (electronic) and designs his own sets (almost always film projections), costumes and props.

Along with Cunningham and Taylor, Nikolais has enjoyed as much success abroad as in the United States, and he, too, has been the recipient of grants to enable him to expand upon his complex theater form.

A principal dancer with Nikolais was Murray Louis, who, while continuing a close artistic association with his teacher, has become an independent choreographer with his own company. Louis, a dancer who moves like mercury and has an astonishing discipline of his body, works in the Nikolais idiom but with his own highly individual choreographic images.

These representatives of the avant-garde, along with others I shall mention, represent the third, and into the fourth and fifth, generations of modern dance. Some elected to continue in the great creative areas opened up by the original modern-dance pioneers, while others—Cunningham, Shearer, Taylor, Nikolais among them—sought out new paths. Both groups have contributed equally to the extension of modern dance, and indeed modern theater, into the future.

But first to others of the avant-garde persuasion. There is a group known as "the Judson Church group," composed of various dancer-choreographers and their individual companies. They are not allied in any way, but they are identified because they have performed in the old Judson Church building on Washington Square in New York. The minister, the Rev. Al Carmines, who is also a composer, began in the 1960's to encourage young dancers with way-out ideas and gave them a hall in his church in which to experiment. These concerts attracted highly sympathetic audiences, were reviewed in the press and helped launch a number of young dance experimenters who subsequently became known on the national dance scene.

Jeff Duncan and his Dance Theatre Workshop, composed of a variety of choreographers, has its headquarters in a loft-studio, although the members have also performed in theaters and concert halls.

Among the most influential of the avant-garde experimenters of the late 1960's and early '70's were Twyla Tharp,

Meredith Monk, Yvonne Rainer, James Waring, Arthur Bauman, Deborah Jowitt (also a dance critic) and, although he belongs to the Limón generation, Erick Hawkins (onetime principal in the Martha Graham Company). Some of these dancers and their colleagues performed in corridors in galleries and museums, along the beach, in lobbies in what might be described as traveling choreography. Occasionally, members of an audience were taken up and propelled into the happenings.

The avant-garde also introduced total nudity to the theater long before Broadway turned up with *Hair* (the first Broadway show to present nude males and females) and *Oh, Calcutta*. Nudity in dance was to be found in works created by East Coast dancers in studios and little theaters in New York and in the West by Ann Halprin and her San Francisco Dancers' Workshop. In one work a nude male soloist, performing on stage within a huge plastic box, placed various parts of his body in pans of paint—white, black, red—and then rubbed against the front plastic curtain, thus creating his own murals without using his hands. In one of her dances Miss Halprin had three men and three women undress, dress and undress on stage and then, while nude, move about in vast rolls of brown wrapping paper.

The modern dance continues to flourish with those who are not classified as avant-garde. On the borderline would be Anna Sokolow, an early member of the Martha Graham Company, and an independent dancer and choreographer since the 1930's. Sokolow, who trained Jeff Duncan among others, has created not only for modern-dance companies but also for ballet troupes, although she does not change her frenetic, jazzy style of movement for either. Her themes touch upon today's world with its loneliness, fear, frenzy and hopelessness. Her dances, then, are not agreeable, but they are powerful and they are truly "modern."

Today's moderns who do not fall into the avant-garde category would include Pauline Koner and Lucas Hoving (once directed by Humphrey) and Pearl Lang, who closely resembles her former teacher, Graham. One of the most successful in this modern-dance area is Norman Walker, whose line of descent from Graham is through two ex-Graham dancers, May O'Donnell, who had her own company for many years, and Gertrude Shurr. Walker, who has a company of his own, also choreographs for other troupes, both modern and ballet. Bella Lewitsky who, like Myra Kinch, does not descend from the modern dance movement of the East Coast, was first a pupil of and then an associate of the late Lester Horton, and later formed her own school and company.

Among the most successful of the youngest generation of moderns are Louis Falco (trained by Limón), a virtuosic dancer (something like his colleague in the Graham company, Robert Powell) and an interesting choreographer, and Lar Lubovitch, who is very possibly the foremost virtuoso of modern dance and one very likely to become a major choreographer for his generation. Young dancers such as these represent a new concept of training, that is, one that differs from that of the 1920's and '30's, for although they specialize in modern dance and choreograph in modern-dance style, they all study ballet assiduously. From this classical training they obtain a technical precision and virtuosity not possible with modern training alone.

The 1940's and '50's were comparatively lean years for modern dancers—there were the occasional concerts, paid for in sweat and poverty, and a living made from teaching or Broadway shows. By the 1960's modern dancers of distinction had not only increased in numbers but were giving more concerts and doing more tours than ever before. Increased public interest in modern and avant-garde dancing accounted for many of these changes, but of paramount importance was the financial aid provided by grants from arts councils and foundations.

Where once the Guggenheim Foundation was the only major foundation to provide grants, mainly token ones, for dance, by the 1960's funds were available from the Ford and Rockefeller Foundations (into the millions of dollars), from the Rebekah Harkness Foundation (chiefly for Harkness dance enterprises), from the Lepercq Foundation and from several other personal foundations. Grants also come from state councils on the arts (every state has an arts council or its equivalent), with New York State having provided the model for all subsequent state councils (the arts budget for New York in 1970–1971 was twenty million dollars).

The councils and the foundations, of course, support ballet as well as other forms of dance.

During the history of modern dance in America not all has been of native make. Mary Wigman, co-founder with Rudolf von Laban of modern dance in Europe, came to America with her company in the early 1930's and shocked, stirred, infuriated and illumined many with her new and challenging art. Harald Kreutzberg came and continued to return over the years—except during World War II—with a partner or alone, to give American audiences generous glimpses of his faultless dancing and his unique characterizations, some macabre, others frothy, still others poetic.

Trudi Schoop and her Comic Ballet also visited America, and a perennial favorite, until after the war when the passage of time made its programs seem sadly dated, was the Jooss Ballet, headed by Kurt Jooss, who worked in a medium which sought to combine elements of traditional ballet and modern dance. In the company's repertory were many ballets which won instant favor, but none was more impressive than the antiwar work *The Green Table,* which became the Jooss trademark and the solid foundation upon which the organization's reputation was built and upon which it rested for many years. Later, *The Green Table* entered the family of classics as it was added to the repertory of other companies, notably the City Center Joffrey Ballet, which restaged it in the 1960's under Jooss's personal direction.

The black American has contributed richly to the dance in America. He has done it on his own and in collaboration with his white colleagues. His position in the field of modern dance is of historic significance, so to look at his contributions in sequence, from colonial days to the present, a chapter on "The Black Dance" reports not only on the story of the Negro in American dance but pinpoints his place in modern dance (as well as in tap, ballet and musical-theater forms) .

12

The Black Dance

They marched "with colors flying and drums beating." They were black slaves, and they had rebelled against their masters in South Carolina and were fighting their way toward a hoped-for freedom in Florida. They never got there. The brief insurrection was quickly put down the very year it began, 1739. A few months later, in 1740, laws were introduced banning any and all blacks from "beating drums" or making any other kinds of noises and sounds which might possibly inflame slaves and propel them toward another rebellion.

The history of American, as distinct from remembered African, black dance may, very possibly, be said to begin with this date. The slaves quickly turned to other percussion devices—clappers made of bone and jawbones among them—and, most important to the evolution of dance in America, footbeats. The Negroes, with their African heritage, had of course danced, but with the magical voice, and soul, of the drum taken away from them, they combined within their own bodies both movement and sound. In time, those with performing talents picked up the white man's clog dancing, and from this logical, but unanticipated dance union, was born the tap dance, the first indigenous American art dance, other than the ritual dances of the American Indian.

The Negro performer was popular, so popular that he was imitated by whites in blackface. The Negro dance boy was a stock type to be seen in any number of variety shows, plays and entertainments. He was to the American stage what "blackamoors" were to European operas and extravaganzas. But the Negro "boy" was not a copy of his European cousin; his rhythms, his steps, his musical instruments, his words mirrored his New World place. It is true that in the late eighteenth and early nineteenth centuries the white man in blackface outnumbered the real Negro. Indeed, the great blackface artist, Daddy Rice (the original Jim Crow), is believed to have been the first performer to use genuine Negro work songs in his act. But star black dancers, and even all-black theatrical troupes, existed as far back as George Washington's administration.

Integration, on stage, was not uncommon. William Henry Lane, a Negro, took for his stage name the title of the popular dance, Juba (from the African *giouba*), and made it famous. By 1850 he had been hailed enthusiastically, and Europe called him "the greatest dancer in the world." He was the black star of an all-white American company, and he was treated as a star. Not only was he praised for the virtuosity of his steps, but his dancing was also described as "beautiful." Juba's nearest rival was a Master John Diamond, who was referred to, understandably, as the King of Diamonds. But in contests with Juba, he lost, and Juba was proclaimed the King of All Dancers.

For most of the nineteenth century the Negro dancer could find a career ranging from saloon entertainment to the best in the enormously popular minstrel shows. After the Civil War his theatrical possibilities in the South were curtailed, but his popularity in the North increased, as it did in Europe. At the turn of the twentieth century, Northern Negroes were creating their own shows: composing the music, writing the book, performing (as dancers, singers, actors), and with great success. Such titles as *Coon Town* or *In Bandana Land* would make today's blacks cringe, but they represented a noteworthy advance over the minstrel-hoofer Negro "boy" or the stock comic with the "fright" wig or even the image of the "ole darkie" happy on "de ole plantation."

It has been in this century, the twentieth, that the African, imported to America as a slave, has found not only his political freedom but also his identity, black but non-African, in the arts. He is aware of his heritage, but he is also concerned with his "now." Thus it is possible to have a Pearl Primus exploring the ancestral dances of Africa; Percival Borde or Jean-Léon Destiné or the great pioneer, Katherine Dunham, delving for dance roots in the Caribbean; some choreographers finding the tools of expression through the technique of America's modern dance; others finding new and unexpected outlets in classical ballet with its purely white, purely European origins.

The great tradition of the Negro hoofer (usually a singer-dancer) has never disappeared. One of the most famous was

Bill (Bojangles) Robinson, who was everywhere loved not only for his superb stage routines but also for his work in the movies, especially with Shirley Temple. There have been matchless jazz dancers, among them Hony Coles, for example; Avon Long, dancer-singer-actor; the Nicholas Brothers, jumping into splits or actually running up the side of a proscenium arch; Pegleg Bates, extraordinary tap dancer with one leg live and one of wood; the much later Sammy Davis, Jr., a total performer who is as electrifying as a dancer as he is as a singer and actor; and a host of others.

But the first black to go into what might be called "art" dancing was Edna Guy, pupil and protégée of Ruth St. Denis in the late 1920's. By 1931 Miss Guy had founded and performed in New York with her Negro Concert Dancers. In the same year, in Chicago, Katherine Dunham opened her school. From there, Miss Dunham, an anthropologist as well as a gifted dancer and a noted beauty, went on to become the most illustrious "art" Negro dancer of the 1930's, '40's and '50's. She appeared in concert, in Broadway shows (*Cabin in the Sky* among them), in movies and in her own revues (*Bal Nègre* was one), and she was on all occasions the choreographer for herself and her dancers.

Another famous black dancer-anthropologist was Pearl Primus, born in Trinidad but raised in the United States. Her initial theatrical training was in modern dance, and in the 1940's her program always contained dances of protest, among them *Strange Fruit* (the subject was lynching). But she began to add danced Negro spirituals to her solo repertory, then dances of Caribbean origin, and finally, with the aid of grants, she was able to travel and study in Africa. With her African experiences, her direction changed, and her subsequent, and continuing, career is rooted in African heritage. Some of her dances, created first for herself and company and later, as she turned to choreography and teaching rather than to dancing, for others, including her husband, the Trinidadian Percival Borde, were absolutely authentic tribal dances, while others were her own creative evolvements of ethnic themes and rhythms.

Donald McKayle, former dancer, choreographs for his own concert dance company, an integrated but primarily black group, for musicals (*Golden Boy,* for one) and for television. His technique is that of modern dance, and his associations, other than as a student of Martha Graham, have been primarily with the New Dance Group Studio in New York. His first successful creation, *Games,* a playful and yet tragic view of tenement children in the streets, was first done in 1951 and is still performed.

On the West Coast the late Lester Horton, white, started a school and company in the late 1920's. Initially, his interest was centered in themes of the American Indian, and he never lost that concern, but through his teaching he began to develop black dancers and to train them up to the highest level of performing. Among these dancers was Janet Collins, a remarkably gifted soloist (she also choreographed her own programs), who made her New York debut in 1949, and who became première danseuse (the first of her race to hold such a post) of the Metropolitan Opera in 1951, remaining with the company until 1954 when she returned to concert work and to teaching.

Other Horton dancers were Collins' cousin, the extraordinarily beautiful and versatile Carmen de Lavallade; James Truitte, dancer and teacher; and Alvin Ailey, who subsequently became the founder-director of the Alvin Ailey American Dance Theater, an integrated company (mainly black) which has toured not only nationally but also, with the sponsorship of the U.S. Department of State, internationally. His choreographic successes are many, including such works as *Blues Suite* (1958), *Roots of the Blues, Revelations, Hermit Songs, Masekela Language* (created in 1969 to songs composed by a black South African, Masekela) and many more. He has also choreographed for companies other than his own (the Joffrey and Harkness ballets), for Broadway shows and for television, and in 1966 created the dances for the new opera, Samuel Barber's *Anthony and Cleopatra,* which opened the new Metropolitan Opera House in New York's Lincoln Center for the Performing Arts. For his company's repertory, Ailey uses works by other choreographers also, both white (Pauline Koner and Joyce Trisler are two) and black (Talley Beatty would be one).

Beatty is a Dunham alumnus who has had a company of his own and occasionally organizes a group for a concert, but many of his creations are in a variety of repertories for both black and white companies. One of his most famous dances is *The Road of the Phoebe Snow,* a ballet about poverty, anger, fear, love and murder in the lives of people living along the railroad tracks. It has been danced by an all-black troupe, by an all-white company and by an integrated dance unit, all with equal success. Beatty is much in demand in Europe, as are other black American dancers, as a teacher and choreographer.

The six-foot-six Geoffrey Holder from Trinidad is not only a dancer and choreographer but also a successful painter, illustrator, author and singer. His choreographic themes are often, although not always, rooted in Caribbean life and lore, and their productions are intensely theatrical, sporting wildly exotic costumes which he designs himself. Sometimes he choreographs for his wife, Carmen de Lavallade, who is herself an accomplished choreographer, or Alvin Ailey or a group of his own dancers. As a dancer, he has appeared not only in concert but on Broadway and with the Metropolitan Opera. The Met, incidentally, fostered black artists long before black pressure called for a fair balance in casting; beginning with Janet Collins, it went on to appoint de Lavallade her successor as première danseuse, and subsequently to engage Katherine Dunham to do the choreography for a new staging of *Aïda* and, of course, Ailey for the gala opening of the new house.

Arthur Mitchell, trained in both ballet and modern dance as a public school pupil in New York City's High School of the Performing Arts, went on to become the first of his race to be ranked as a premier danseur in classical ballet. Oddly, Mitchell's major was modern dance rather than ballet—he later was an important member of a modern dance company directed by John Butler—but with continuing ballet studies, he perfected his technique to become, ultimately, a principal dancer with the New York City Ballet. George Balanchine, the company's director, created roles especially for his talents, among them Puck in the ballet version of *A Midsummer Night's Dream.*

In 1968 Mitchell began teaching in New York's vast

Negro subcommunity, Harlem, and in 1969 established the Dance Theatre of Harlem, the first classical Negro ballet company in history. The repertory, of course, is not exclusively classical in tone—there are jazz ballets and rituals evocative of an African heritage—for as in other contemporary ballet companies, innovations and variety of style are as important as the continuation of the most rigid standards of the *ballet d'école*. As a dancer, Mitchell himself has a similar range: as a guest artist with the Metropolitan Opera, he has danced with the French-born ballerina, Violette Verdy, in Gluck's *Orfeo ed Euridice,* and in the New York City Ballet's production of Balanchine's *Slaughter on Tenth Avenue* (originally in the musical *On Your Toes*) he is called upon to do loose-hipped jazz.

Among other black graduates of the School of the Performing Arts are the dancer-choreographer Eleo Pomare and William Louther, a virtuosic performer who appeared with several mostly black companies and with the Martha Graham Company. Miss Graham has long had an integrated company, including Orientals as well as blacks. Louther, Dudley Williams and Clive Thompson have been important in the male wing, and on the female side Mary Hinkson and Matt Turney have been outstanding. Both have had major dances created especially for them, and Miss Hinkson, in 1969, was selected to dance the role originated by Miss Graham herself nearly thirty years before in *Deaths and Entrances.*

Negro ballet schools are growing, and classes in modern dance, Afro forms, ethnic studies and jazz taught by black teachers are to be found in Europe and the American South as well as the North. In Africa itself new pride is being taken in the ancient tribal dances, and efforts are being made to retain their purity on the one hand and to translate them into theatrical terms on the other. America has helped in both these enterprises. A government official of Ghana came to the Juilliard School in New York to study Labanotation, the most accurate dance script yet devised, in order to return to his homeland and record tribal dances before they had become corrupted by outside influences. Pearl Primus, under the sponsorship of the government of Liberia, established a dance center in that country and with the aid of American funds journeyed into the newly independent nations of Africa, where she advised on the establishment of arts centers, dance training programs, auditioning tribal dancers, and on how to adapt native dances to the stage.

American blacks, two hundred and more years after their uprising against slavery, are still with their "colors flying and drums beating." But during the course of those two centuries they have built, in America, not only a black dance but, more important, an art dance that belongs to and has enriched the whole world of dance.

13

American Ballet Is Born

The birth (or rebirth) of American ballet in the twentieth century owes much to a woman (which seems natural), to a ballerina from Russia (which seems odd). Nevertheless, it was the immortal Anna Pavlova who revived America's slumbering interest in ballet and who, through her numerous coast-to-coast tours of the country, helped to establish ballet as a delightful, artistic, enduring form of theater.

After *The Black Crook* and its successors had faded from memory, little of any importance was left of ballet in America. With the establishment of the Metropolitan Opera in 1883, opera ballet took on some semblance of permanence, but for several years the dancers were importations and when the time came for the building of opera ballet with resident talent, not much that is memorable came from the venture.

Attempts were made at the Metropolitan and by the short-lived American Opera Company to give the country, or at least New York, good ballet, but interest in the art had sunk so low that a half-century period of balletic decline in America did not end until the great Danish ballerina Adeline Genée entranced New York in 1908 and Pavlova literally electrified the metropolitan public when she made her local debut two years later.

Genée was first seen by New Yorkers in a musical, *The Soul Kiss*, but in 1912, at the Metropolitan, she appeared in an all-ballet production, *La Danse*, a program in which she sought to recreate the dance characteristics of great ballerinas of the past. Until her retirement in 1917, Genée shuttled between London, her home and the scene of her greatest triumphs, and America, where her lightness, delicacy and piquant style found favor with the American public.

Pavlova's American debut was made at the Metropolitan in *Coppélia*, in which she and Mikhail Mordkin danced with the support of the resident corps de ballet. Success was instantaneous. The great ballerina and the virile Mordkin appeared also in various pas de deux throughout the season in New York and performances elsewhere. Such was the acclaim that they were invited to return the following year with their own company for another New York season and an extended tour of the country.

With the outbreak of the war in Europe, Pavlova assembled a company in England and began her arduous tours of North and South America, expanding her areas of conquest, at the end of hostilities, to the entire world, Russia excepted. From 1910 through her last tour of America in 1925 (she was booked to return in 1931, the year she died of pneumonia in the Netherlands), Pavlova and ballet were pretty nearly synonymous terms to the majority of Americans.

An array of partners—she split with Mordkin after their second American season—came and went, but Pavlova and her company continued to dance in opera houses, auditoriums, movie theaters, schools, vaudeville houses across the land. To audiences, she brought such classics as *Giselle* as well as the famed *Dying Swan,* created for her by Fokine. Her repertory was huge, but in spite of her early association with Fokine and his rebellious ideas she was basically a traditionalist. There were, admittedly, examples of Oriental-style dances among her productions, but the classic technique was her forte.

Most of the critics and historians of the Pavlova era felt that the choreographies she used were, with few exceptions, inferior. The quality of her dancing, however, never dropped below the incredibly high standard of perfection she set for herself. With a perfect dancer's body—strong and slim legs, long and lovely arms, an arching neck, exquisitely poised hands, a finely modeled torso—and a carefully schooled technique which made the difficult appear easy, she was able to flood her dances with that intangible combination of beauty and power which we may call genius.

As a dancer, Pavlova was something of a teacher, for through her dancing she taught Americans to love and to respect the ballet. How many dreams she created in the imaginations of little girls and what ambitions for their children she stirred in the minds of doting mothers cannot be estimated. But because of Pavlova, Americans not only attended the ballet but many wanted to become a part of it.

Now, long after her death, her image and her legend remain sharply etched on the American ballet scene, for although she left no new schools of dance movement, no major ballet creations behind her, and although her dancing genius died with her, the symbol of her perfection remained, and perhaps always will, a guide and a goal to the female student of ballet and to ballerinas of other generations as well.

In 1916 came another Russian invasion, this time in the form of the great Diaghilev company, which had roused Western Europe out of its ballet lethargy in 1909 at its Paris debut. Here was ballet quite different from that offered by Pavlova. Here was ballet built upon the new principles evolved by Fokine and continued by others. Here was ballet at its most modern, bright, lavish, sophisticated.

Neither of Diaghilev's most famous stars, Nijinsky (interned in Hungary) nor Karsavina (performing in London), came with the troupe, but the American season was an artistic success despite financial and temperamental difficulties. *Petrouchka, Les Sylphides, Scheherazade* (all by Fokine) and Nijinsky's controversial *Afternoon of a Faun* (danced by Massine) were among the colorful productions given. Earlier, New York had seen unauthorized versions of three Fokine ballets staged by Gertrude Hoffman.

Later in 1916, Nijinsky arrived in America and, with a company of Diaghilev dancers, toured through 1917, creating his last ballet, *Till Eulenspiegel,* in this land. Although Mordkin had won unstinting praise for his dancing with Pavlova, Nijinsky, hailed as the greatest male dancer in Europe, earned equal accolades here. His phenomenal leaps, his animal strength, his unquestioned artistry proved that legends from abroad were facts.

But things were happening fast in America. Nijinsky and

the Diaghilev company departed, never to return. Mordkin, a choreographer as well as a dancer, ultimately turned to teaching and, late in his life, to producing. Adolph Bolm, who had headed the Diaghilev company on its first American tour, remained to form his own ballet company, and in the early 1920's Fokine made America his home. Pavlova, Diaghilev and Nijinsky had opened up new ballet territory in America, and ballet leaders from the Old World were ready to start their extended pioneering duties in the New World.

Still, there was a sporadic nature to ballet enterprise in America until 1933, the year the Ballet Russe de Monte Carlo came to America for a brief New York season and a tour, both artistically successful but financially near-disastrous. But S. Hurok, the impresario who had brought the Ballet Russe to America, knew that America was ready for continuing seasons of ballet whether America knew it or not. The Ballet Russe de Monte Carlo returned again and again and became, in a few years, an American institution, its name to the contrary.

The Ballet Russe, heir to the Diaghilev company (Diaghilev had died in 1929 and the dancers had been scattered), had Colonel Wassily de Basil as its director; Leonide Massine, chief choreographer; Alexandra Danilova, senior ballerina; and the three so-called "baby ballerinas," Tamara Toumanova, Irina Baronova and Tatiana Riabouchinska. In its initial American seasons the company offered a repertory which included productions from the Diaghilev days and new ballets by Massine, among them his symphonic ballets, such as *Les Présages* (Tchaikovsky's Fifth), *Choreartium,* which employed a good deal of modern-dance actions (Brahms's

Fourth) and Berlioz' *Symphonie Fantastique*. Later symphonic ballet by Massine were *Labyrinth* (Schubert's Seventh), *Seventh Symphony* (Beethoven) and *Rouge et Noir* (Shostakovitch's First). There were lighter Massine works also, among them the enduring *Le Beau Danube* and the ever-popular *Gaîté Parisienne*.

Russian ballet in America appeared to be doing splendidly. The Metropolitan Opera House, beginning in 1935, became the annual site for a ballet opening as prestige-laden, or almost, as that previously reserved for opera and symphony. But a war was on within the Ballet Russe de Monte Carlo itself, and in 1938 the company split, with de Basil heading one unit and Massine the other.

Although de Basil kept his company going for many years after the separation, finding new stars and choreographers, playing rival seasons with the Ballet Russe de Monte Carlo (under Massine) in London and New York, touring the world and functioning under several names, the most familiar being the Original Ballet Russe, it was the Massine company, retaining the parent name, that established itself permanently.

By 1940 Massine had assembled an enviable roster of stars. Danilova, Alicia Markova and Mia Slavenska were the ballerinas, and the impressive male wing was headed by Igor Youskevitch, André Eglevsky and Frederic Franklin. (For a period de Basil could boast the "baby ballerinas" and David Lichine and Anton Dolin.) But there never was any constancy in matters of personnel. Stars and soloists came and went, joined other companies, took on guest-artist duties, formed their own dance groups, and only the confirmed balletomane or careful historian could keep track of who was in which company when.

Danilova, however, remained loyal to the Ballet Russe de Monte Carlo, and her appearances with the same organization year after year in New York and across the nation established her as a ballerina known and loved by a vast public. Indeed, so closely associated was she with the art of ballet itself that a spontaneous ovation greeted her one evening at the Metropolitan as she came on stage for her role as the Glove Seller in *Gaîté Parisienne,* an ovation which stopped the performance for several minutes, had the ballerina in tears and became, in ensuing seasons, an annual manifestation of public tribute to the dancer and to the effervescent *Gaîté* with which she has always been associated.

Eventually, Massine withdrew from the Ballet Russe, and the company continued to function, with many ups and downs, under the direction of Serge Denham. As the years wore on, the Ballet Russe, despite the continuing artistry of Danilova and Franklin, began to wane. It became primarily a touring company featuring aging productions of such old-time favorites as *Scheherazade, The Nutcracker* and *Swan Lake,* and Massine's *Gaîté* and *Danube.*

New works were, of course, produced, but after a short association with George Balanchine in the mid-1940's, when the great choreographer staged some of his finest ballets for this company, the choreographic level of the company was often substandard. The first five years of the 1950's found the Ballet Russe skirting New York, playing at the Lewisohn Stadium but not Broadway. Under the booking management of Columbia Artists, and in an effort to bolster the company's prestige, Maria Tallchief was engaged as prima ballerina (with a year's leave from her home company, the New York City Ballet) at the unheard-of sum of two thousand dollars a week.

For the 1955–1956 season, Alicia Alonso and Youskevitch, formerly with the Ballet Theatre, were engaged as stars, but still the Ballet Russe remained a touring company. Of the permanent stars, only Franklin and Leon Danielian remained, for Danilova had left a few years before to form her own ballet unit, to make guest appearances and to teach in a large school in Texas.

If, by 1956, the former magic of the Ballet Russe de Monte Carlo was sadly dim, its box-office appeal on the road remained high. Weariness of constantly touring performers, budgetary problems, poor casting, lack of a creative plan, faulty artistic direction and any of a number of difficulties could have contributed to the decline. However, the Ballet Russe de Monte Carlo established ballet in America on a permanent, professional basis; produced Massine's finest works, enriched its repertory with many ballets by Balanchine and kept the old classics and the Fokine masterpieces before the public; introduced the most glittering of ballet stars to the public and, with the production of such ballets as Agnes de Mille's *Rodeo,* focused international attention upon the successful use of American folk themes in ballet and, incidentally, helped in changing the course of the popular theater, for from *Rodeo* de Mille went on to create her history-making dances in *Oklahoma!*

Thirty years after its dazzling New York debut, the Ballet

Russe de Monte Carlo, faded, weary and all but forgotten, ceased to exist.

While the Ballet Russe de Monte Carlo was making its American debut in 1933, two young Americans, Lincoln Kirstein and Edward M. M. Warburg, were completing plans for the establishment of the School of American Ballet in Hartford, Connecticut, under the direction of Balanchine and Vladimir Dimitriew (a former singer of the Maryinsky Theater in Leningrad). But plans were changed and the new school actually opened its doors in New York City on the first day of 1934.

The founders envisioned the school as a training ground for American dancers and choreographers, the home from which a performing company might one day step forth. That Russians were the preparers of American ballet seemed perfectly logical to Kirstein, for the ancient tradition of ballet had reached its peak in Russia, and in Balanchine, Kirstein had found not only a great choreographer but also a sensitive teacher-director eager to apply and adapt Russian training methods to American bodies and American temperaments and eager also to create ballets for the as yet unjelled American style of ballet.

In the fall of the same year, a performing unit of the school made its debut in Hartford in a repertory of four ballets, all of them by Balanchine, one a comedy on an American theme. In March of 1935 the American Ballet, with guest artists augmenting its semiprofessional students, made its New York debut at the Adelphi Theater in an engagement extended from one week to two.

The season was a success, although differences of opinion among the critics arose, and there seemed every reason to go on. But where? Bookings for the new company, which did not have a "Russe" in its name to help it along, were not easy to come by. Therefore, it was something in the nature of manna from heaven when the Metropolitan Opera invited the American Ballet to become the resident company at the opera.

The association lasted from 1935 to 1938, and it was not an entirely happy one. Balanchine paid no attention to the old and exhausted opera-ballet traditions and proceeded to create entirely new and, at that time, avant-garde dances for the opera. Old-timers fumed at his opera ballets, his independent ballets and his revolutionary staging of Gluck's *Orfeo*. Balanchine, for the needs of opera at least, was ahead of his time, and the union of the Metropolitan Opera and the American Ballet could not last.

Kirstein, meanwhile, launched another ballet plan. In the summer of 1936 he formed the Ballet Caravan, composed of some dancers from the American Ballet and others from the school. This little company was not to have the benefit of Balanchine choreography, for its purpose was to present American dancers in ballets choreographed by novice American choreographers. Eugene Loring, Lew Christensen and William Dollar, all destined to make their marks as mature choreographers, were among those represented in the debut program at Bennington College in Vermont and on the subsequent tour.

In the fall the Caravan dancers rejoined the mother company at the Metropolitan and did not set out for a second season until 1938, when Loring's *Yankee Clipper* and Christensen's *Filling Station,* along with several other ballets, were added to the repertory. A successful New York engagement highlighted the Caravan's year, and in the autumn it produced what was to become one of the most popular of all American ballets, Loring's *Billy the Kid.*

In 1939 the American Ballet went out of existence; the following year the Ballet Caravan was disbanded. But both companies enjoyed a joint rebirth as the American Ballet Caravan in 1941, when a goodwill tour of Latin America was arranged by Nelson Rockefeller, then heading a State Department agency devoted to cultural relations among the American republics.

Pooling repertories of the two companies and adding new works, the group set out with a repertory which included Balanchine's *Ballet Imperial, Concerto Barocco, The Bat, Errante, Serenade* and *Apollo,* as well as ballets by Loring, Christensen, Dollar and one by Antony Tudor. With the completion of this six-month tour, the American Ballet and the Ballet Caravan ended their service forever.

The school kept going and growing, and the dancers found jobs in Hollywood, in other ballet companies, on Broadway, in their own little organizations. It was not until 1946 that Balanchine and Kirstein again took up the interrupted work of creating the American ballet company they had dreamed about thirteen years before. The new project was called Ballet Society, an organization dedicated to the producton of new works for the lyric theater, publication of dance literature, producton of dance films and related activities. Performances were to be open to members only.

In November, 1946, Ballet Society offered *The Spellbound Child* (Ravel), an opera fantasy, and *The Four Temperaments* (Hindemith), a straight ballet, both choreographed by Balanchine. Later productions included Balanchine's *Divertimento* (Haieff) and Merce Cunningham's *The Seasons* (John Cage), as well as two operas, *The Medium* and *The Telephone. The Triumph of Bacchus and Ariadne,* a ballet cantata to music of Vittorio Rieti, and two of the best ballets Balanchine produced for Ballet Society, *Symphonie Concertante* (Mozart) and *Symphony in C* (Bizet), followed.

But Ballet Society was a far too exciting organization to keep from the general public. Furthermore, it had its problems in finding places to perform. Finally, after a series of performances at the New York City Center of Music and Drama, the directors asked Kirstein if he would like a permanent home for his company, and in 1948 the New York City Ballet was born.

The first season, following on top of an engagement by the star-laden Ballet Russe de Monte Carlo, played to pleased but small audiences. Maria Tallchief, formerly a soloist of the Ballet Russe, had long since made a deep impression on ballet followers, and in 1947 had become the first American ballerina since the time of Augusta Maywood to dance with the Paris Opéra. But Tallchief was not yet a popular favorite, a household word with the general public.

In the ensuing years, however, the New York City Ballet grew into one of the world's major ballet companies. As artistic director, Balanchine has supplied most of the repertory, turning out with undiminished zeal and inventiveness everything from program-long ballets through purely musical ballets and dramatic works to brief, flashing pas de deux. With the coming of Jerome Robbins, formerly of the Ballet Theatre, as associate artistic director for a period of time, the repertory was wonderfully strengthened by ballets on contemporary themes, modern in style and, for the most part, highly dramatic.

In the late 1960's Robbins returned as a choreographer to create abstract ballets to music of Chopin (two ballets) and Bach. Jacques d'Amboise, premier danseur, was given opportunities to choreograph, as was another young company member, John Clifford. But the repertory remains almost wholly Balanchine.

In its first season at the New York City Center the company played only sixteen performances. Twenty years later it was playing to capacity houses in its new home, the New York State Theater at Lincoln Center (the New York City Ballet opened this theater designed for dance in 1964), for twenty-two weeks of the year.

Most, but not all, of the City Ballet dancers came from the School of American Ballet, and they still do. For years Tallchief was the prima ballerina, with André Eglevsky as the premier danseur. Other stars, over the years, have included Tanaquil LeClercq, Diana Adams, Patricia Wilde, Janet Reed (all now retired) and Melissa Hayden, Allegra Kent and, for several years a Balanchine protégée, Suzanne Farrell; d'Amboise, Arthur Mitchell and Edward Villella, who has become as famous in concert, in musicals and on TV as he has in his home company.

The third of the American ballet companies, the Ballet Theatre, sprang almost full-blown onto the American scene.

Unlike the Ballet Russe de Monte Carlo, which came from abroad, and the New York City Ballet, which evolved from the School of American Ballet and increasingly important preliminary ballet groups, the Ballet Theatre had far from elaborate antecedents and most of those it discarded before it made its historical debut in 1940. (It is now called the American Ballet Theatre.)

In 1937 the performing desires of the advanced students of Mikhail Mordkin's school in New York found satisfaction in the establishment of the Mordkin Ballet, which received substantial financial aid from one of Mordkin's major students, Lucia Chase. The little company expanded, adding important dancers to its roster, but still it was showing no signs of evolving quickly into a first-rank ballet organization.

In the summer of 1939 the formation of the Ballet Theatre took place, and Richard Pleasant was named director with Chase as a guiding force in its organizing. In six months, an incredibly short space of time for such a project, a company had been built, a repertory assembled and created and the debut accomplished with considerable *réclame* at New York's Center Theatre (since torn down) in Rockefeller Center.

The evening opened with a performance of *Les Sylphides* which has since become legend. The corps was trained to perfection, the costumes gloriously fresh, and when Karen Conrad executed in her solo variation the series of diagonal leaps across the stage, the audience gasped unbelievingly, for it seemed as if the high-flying dancer had traversed the great expanse in something like two soaring jumps. This could not have been true, but the impression of aerial brilliance was well founded. Here was a European ballet, but here also was

Tatiana Riabouchinska in *Le Coq d'Or*. (Maurice Seymour)

Alexandra Danilova and Leonide Massine in *Gaîté Parisienne*. (Alfredo Valente)

Anton Dolin and Irina Baronova in *Bluebeard*. (Alfredo Valente)

Tamara Toumanova. (Maurice Seymour)

Frederic Franklin rehearsing at Jacob's Pillow. (Dwight Godwin)

Jacques d'Amboise in *Scotch Symphony*. (Martha Swope)

Edward Villella in *Prince Igor*. (Martha Swope)

Alicia Alonso and Igor Youskevitch in *Giselle*.

Carla Fracci and Erick Bruhn in *Giselle*, American Ballet Theatre. (Martha Swope)

Hugh Laing, Nora Kaye and Antony Tudor in *Lilac Garden*.

Rudolf Nureyev and Margot Fonteyn in *Swan Lake*, Royal Ballet. (Mira)

Arthur Mitchell (Puck) in *A Midsummer Night's Dream,* New York City Ballet. (Martha Swope)

The Boston Ballet with Edward Villella and Violette Verdy as guest stars in *Giselle.* (Frank Derbas)

Tanaquil LeClercq and Jacques
d'Amboise in *Western Symphony*.
(Radford Bascome)

The American Ballet Theatre's production
of Agnes de Mille's *Rodeo*. (Roger Wood)

Harold Lang, Jerome Robbins, John Kriza,
the original sailors of *Fancy Free*.

Richard Cragun as Petruchio in *The
Taming of the Shrew*, Stuttgart Ballet.

Edward Villella and Allegra Kent (center) in *Bugaku*, New York City Ballet. (Martha Swope)

Christine Sarry in *Cortège Parisienne*, Eliot Feld's American Ballet Company. (Ron Protas)

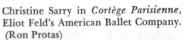

Maria Tallchief with Francisco Moncion in *Firebird*. (George Platt Lynes)

Above left, Raisa Struchkova and Alexander Lipauri in *La Valse*, Bolshoi Ballet. (Martha Swope)

Alicia Markova as she appeared in the Metropolitan Opera's *Orfeo ed Euridice*, by Gluck. (Radford Bascome)

Allegra Kent as the Sugar Plum Fairy in *The Nutcracker*, New York City Ballet. (Martha Swope)

Cynthia Gregory, American Ballet
Theatre. (Ron Protas)

Marcia Haydée in John Cranko's *Romeo and Juliet* (Stuttgart Ballet)

Reginald Laubin, specialist in the dances of
the American Indian.

Jean-Léon Destiné.

Pearl Primus.

Katherine Dunham.

The late Carmen Amaya.
(Friedman-Abeles)

The late Argentinita (with her sister, Pilar Lopez) in the Peruvian *Huayno*. (Alfredo Valente)

José Greco and members of his company.
(Arnold Eagle)

Antonio.

La Meri in an Arabian dance.

Uday Shankar.

Les Ballets Africains (from the Republic of Guinea).

na Enters in *Pavana—Spain, 16th Century*.

Ballet Folklorico of Mexico.

Bayanihan, Philippine Dance Compa

Summer, Moiseyev Dance Company.

Male dancers, in invisible black, support Jackie Gregory on a Danny Kaye show. (CBS Television)

Electronic-TV ballet, Tony Charmoli, choreographer. (William Claxton)

The Radio City Music Hall Rockettes, photographed from backstage as they face their audience. (Radford Bascome)

Revival of *Annie Get Your Gun*, Lincoln Center, 1966. (Frank Derbas)

Russ Tamblyn and other dancers in the movie, *Seven Brides for Seven Brothers*, choreographed by Michael Kidd.

Dan Dailey, Michael Kidd and Gene Kelly in *It's Always Fair Weather*, a movie.

BENESH

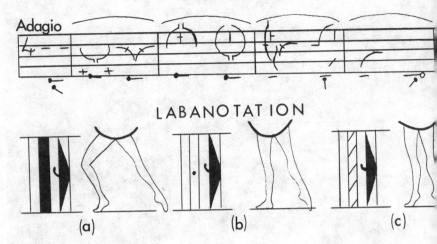

LABANOTATION

(a)   (b)   (c)

Two forms of dance script: top, the Benesh system, a recent method approved by Britain's Royal Ballet. Below, Labanotation, used around the world and invented by Rudolf von Laban, Germany's most famous modern dance pioneer. The vertical notation symbols indicate the movements sketched beside them.

Dancers of tomorrow! Joseph Carow of the New Jersey Ballet teaches single *tours en l'air* to boys of Montclair Junior High School, Montclair, New Jersey. (Frank Derbas)

an American dancer bringing a heritage of big movement and healthy athleticism to ballet. Some would maintain that sylphs should be more delicate and Europeans would also question what they called our "acrobatics," but in this first ballet a dancer had injected American flavor into an international form. The Ballet Theatre was American.

In its initial seasons Pleasant and Chase divided the company into three wings. Anton Dolin was responsible for the classical ballets, Eugene Loring for the American and Antony Tudor for the English. All three were represented in the repertory as choreographers, but the ambitious young company also called on the services of Mordkin, Bolm, Agnes de Mille, Bronislava Nijinska, Andrée Howard (from England), Massine, Fokine and others. It seemed as if only Balanchine were missing.

The principal dancers of the opening season—Patricia Bowman, Chase, Conrad, Nina Stroganova, Viola Essen, Annabelle Lyon, Dolin, Bolm, Danielian, Hugh Laing, Yurek Shabelevsky, Leon Varkas, Dimitri Romanoff, Loring, Tudor and others—were augmented in subsequent seasons and during the company's first years by Alicia Markova, Irina Baronova, Nana Gollner, Rosella Hightower, Sono Osato and other stellar or featured artists who came and went. In the ranks were some promising youngsters, Nora Kaye, Jerome Robbins, John Kriza, Alicia Alonso, Donald Saddler and Muriel Bentley, who were to go on to fame in the world of dance.

The early years were not easy. Critics and dance followers were excited about the Ballet Theatre, and audiences which attended appeared to be enthusiastic. But how to get audi-

ences to come? What did the title "Ballet Theatre" mean? As
Kirstein had discovered, ballet to most Americans meant
Russian ballet, and the public, apparently, couldn't bring
itself to believe that American ballet was worth much. When
the Ballet Theatre, following some artistically vital seasons
with large gaps between engagements the rule rather than
the exception, went under the management of S. Hurok, the
wily impresario billed his new clients as Ballet Theatre but
identified the company, in much larger print, as "THE
GREATEST IN RUSSIAN BALLET." Much to everyone's chagrin, it
worked, and the supporters of American ballet had to agree
that the time was not yet ripe to sell American ballet as
American ballet.

The Ballet Theatre was, of course, American with an
international repertory, but for years many people outside
metropolitan areas thought it was a Russian ballet and that
they must, therefore, be getting their money's worth. One
lady in the Midwest stoutly maintained that she had never
seen the Ballet Theatre, although she described a Ballet
Theatre program and personnel accurately, asserting that she
had only seen "that Russian ballet."

Eventually, the "Russian" designation was dropped as the
American public discovered that ballet was not necessarily
Russian, that it was an international dance form and that
Americans had as much business being in ballet as any other
nationality.

The Ballet Theatre's repertory, indeed, was not Russian,
although it did contain some of the best examples of Russian
ballet. Over the years the Ballet Theatre developed what was
probably the most varied repertory of any ballet company

anywhere in the world. It produced *La Fille Mal Gardée,* created in 1786 by Dauberval, and, in addition to this, the oldest of still extant ballets, it included in its classical wing *Giselle, Swan Lake* (in the one-act version), *Princess Aurora* (the last act of *The Sleeping Beauty*) and various classical pas de deux.

The Diaghilev period was represented by Fokine's *Les Sylphides* and *Petrouchka,* and later Fokine, Massine and Lichine creations were incorporated in the repertory. Balanchine and Dolin were also given representation, but one of the strongest wings was reserved for England's Antony Tudor. The Tudor ballets numbered *Lilac Garden, Pillar of Fire, Dark Elegies, Dim Lustre, Romeo and Juliet, Undertow, Gala Performance, The Judgment of Paris,* and it was in *Pillar of Fire* that Nora Kaye became a star overnight.

But the Ballet Theatre was by no means all Tudor. In 1944 one of the young dancers in the company was allowed to try his hand at choreography, and his first work was an instantaneous and lasting hit. It was called *Fancy Free.* Its creator was Jerome Robbins. Other Robbins ballets followed, among them *Interplay* (first choreographed for a Broadway revue) and *Facsimile,* before he moved on to broader fame as a choreographer of innumerable Broadway successes.

Agnes de Mille was also a creative force in the Ballet Theatre's impressive American wing. Her *Rodeo* was included in the repertory, and so also were *Three Virgins and a Devil, Tally-Ho!, Fall River Legend* and *The Harvest According.* Loring's *Billy the Kid* and Michael Kidd's *On Stage!* were still other American-style ballets by American choreographers. A contemporary French ballet section was added with the coming of the noted French dancer Jean Babilée to the company for a brief period. *Le Jeune Homme et la Mort, L'Amour et Son Amour* and *Les Demoiselles de la Nuit* broadened the range of the repertory still further.

In later years the American Ballet Theatre, while continuing to foster new choreographers, added full-length ballet classics to its repertory. These included a lavish four-act production of *Swan Lake,* staged by David Blair of England's Royal Ballet, described by many critics as the best production of the old Petipa-Ivanov-Tchaikovsky classic to be found anywhere. Blair also did a new *Giselle* for the company, and *Coppélia* was remounted in its full three acts. Robbins created a wholly new version of Stravinsky's *Les Noces* for the company, and new choreographers were launched, among them Michael Smuin, whose first ballet was *Pulcinella Variations,* and Eliot Feld, whose *Harbinger* (1967) caused him to be described as the greatest choreographic find since Jerome Robbins.

(In 1968 Feld left to form his own troupe, the American Ballet Company, which immediately became the resident ballet company at the Brooklyn Academy of Music. The repertory included some non-Feld dances, but most of the ballets were choreographed by the prolific young man who was, on occasion, to be found working on four ballets at a time.)

Among the American Ballet Theatre's stars, both native and imported, in the years after Kaye retired and Alicia Alonso had returned to her native Cuba, were Toni Lander and Erik Bruhn (from Denmark), Carla Fracci from Italy, and Natalia Makarova from Russia (Makarova, a ballerina of the Kirov Ballet, formerly the Maryinsky, in Leningrad, defected to the West in the fall of 1970 while the Soviet troupe was playing in London, and selected Ballet Theatre as her new company), Ivan Nagy (also a defector) from Hungary; and Lupe Serrano, Cynthia Gregory, Royes Fernandez, Bruce Marks (a modern dancer turned to ballet), Ted Kivitt, Eleanor d'Antuono, Sallie Wilson (who inherited the Kaye roles), Feld (until he left in 1968), Smuin and many more.

The New York City Ballet's choreographic strength is, of course, centered in the works of Balanchine. He, too, has given his repertory full-length works, starting with his enormously popular staging of *The Nutcracker* and continuing with *Don Quixote, A Midsummer Night's Dream* and *The Jewels.* His long association with Stravinsky culminated in one of the great short ballets of the century, *Agon* (1957), and many other works by this man who has been hailed as the choreographic genius of the twentieth century were cast in that form in which he is unequaled: the extending of musical forms, shapes, rhythms and dynamics into movement.

In addition to the New York City Ballet, the American Ballet Theatre and the American Ballet Company, the nation by the mid-1960's had two more major ballet troupes. These were one headed by the choreographer-teacher-director, Robert Joffrey, and one sponsored by a wealthy patroness of the arts, Rebekah Harkness. Joffrey, a successful young dancer, established his first group in 1954. In 1962 the Rebekah Harkness Foundation assumed support of the Joffrey Ballet, an association terminated in 1964. After a year of reorganization the Joffrey Ballet was reconstituted and in 1966 became the City Center Joffrey Ballet, resident company at the New York City Center. Gerald Arpino has been the associate director and chief choreographer, and has created a series of widely acclaimed ballets: *Viva Vivaldi!*, *Olympics*, *Trinity* (a rock ballet) , *Sea Shadow*, *Clowns* and other successes.

When Mrs. Harkness withdrew her foundation's support from Joffrey, she retained under contract many of the principal dancers and, in 1964, formed the Harkness Ballet. This new company developed into one of the major ballet troupes in the world. Its repertory included a great many works in modern style, among them ballets by Norman Walker, Brian Macdonald, Alvin Ailey, John Butler, Stuart Hodes, Agnes de Mille, George Skibine (the company's first of several directors) . In 1965 Harkness House for Ballet Arts was established in New York City. Subsequently, trainees from this school were formed into a group called the Harkness Youth Dancers. In 1969 Mrs. Harkness disbanded the enormously successful Harkness Ballet and gave her support to the Youth Dancers, a group which was given the name Harkness Ballet Company.

Earlier, the Philadelphia Ballet was founded by Catherine Littlefield in 1935 with Miss Littlefield as the chief choreographer and star dancer. Although the company produced one of the first full-length stagings of *The Sleeping Beauty* to be seen in America (1937) , its popularity, both here and during a London season, derived from contemporary ballets such as *Barn Dance* and *Terminal*. After five years of activity, during which she choreographed, danced, directed and participated in the building of ballet in America, Miss Littlefield turned her talents to ice shows and, until her death, specialized in creating ballets for skaters.

To chronicle fully Ruth Page's activities in the field of American dance would require a volume, for her long career has led her into all sorts of dance associations, experiences and accomplishments. She danced briefly with the Pavlova and the Diaghilev companies, she turned to modern dance for two seasons as Harald Kreutzberg's partner, she was a member of the Adolph Bolm Ballet Intime, she toured as a soloist, she headed several different ballet companies, she participated in the Federal Theater Project and she has been a prolific choreographer for herself, her own dance groups, opera companies and ballet companies both here and abroad.

Narrowing her many achievements down to the field of American ballet, one can note that in 1937 she joined with Bentley Stone in the formation of the Page-Stone Ballet Company. Making Chicago her headquarters, Page served her city as ballet mistress and choreographer for the various Chicago opera enterprises for more than thirty years. Between opera ballet seasons, Page and Stone took their company on the road, bringing contemporary ballet to cities and towns across the country.

Together, Page and Stone created the highly successful *Frankie and Johnny,* which ultimately found a home in the repertory of the Ballet Russe de Monte Carlo, and *Guns and Castanets,* derived from the opera *Carmen.* Other opera-inspired ballets by Page were *Revenge (Il Trovatore)* and

The Merry Widow, the former produced by the Ballets des Champs Élysées in Paris, the latter by the London Festival Ballet.

The Bells, Billy Sunday and almost countless other full-scale ballets, shorter works, divertissements, duets and solos add up to an enormous personal repertory. Not all of the Page ballets have been good. Some have been mediocre, some downright bad, others challenging. But imagination, invention, daring and vitality have marked her extraordinary career and she has been, for well over half a century, an important figure on the American dance scene.

In the nation's West, regional ballet has flowered best in San Francisco. Just as 1933 was a key year for ballet in New York, so it was for ballet in San Francisco. That year the San Francisco Opera Ballet, headed by Adolph Bolm, was born and the associated opera-ballet school founded.

For three seasons, Bolm served as ballet master and choreographer for the company in its duties with the San Francisco Opera and director of the school. Next came Serge Oukrainsky in 1936 to take over the job and with him, as premier danseur, was Willam Christensen. Two years later, in 1938, Willam was made director and the family of dancing Christensens found a new realm. In 1940 Harold joined his brother in San Francisco, and in 1948 Lew gave up his various activities with the Balanchine-Kirstein ballet enterprises to give San Francisco a ballet triumvirate of Christensens.

Under Willam, such classics as *Coppélia, Swan Lake* and *The Nutcracker* were produced, and with the arrival of Lew, *Filling Station, Con Amore* (both popular productions in the repertory of the New York City Ballet), *A Masque of*

Beauty and the Shepherd, Le Gourmand, Heuriger and other ballets were added over the years. Because of an exchange program with the New York City Ballet, the San Francisco Ballet has been able to enrich its repertory with several Balanchine works.

Under two Christensens, Lew and Harold (Willam left in 1951 to head the ballet department at the University of Utah), the San Francisco Ballet stands as one of the nation's major companies. It has left behind its local-only status, and has become a company of national and international renown. World tours, under the auspices of the U.S. Department of State, highlighted its activities in the 1950's.

There are and will be other regional ballet centers in America, but to Philadelphia, Chicago and San Francisco go the honors for building American ballet outside of New York on an artistic level higher than one would have believed possible, ballet materials (especially personnel) being on a scanty basis during the pioneering years.

It was not an easy birth, the creation of American ballet, but the new child of the American theater thrived. And as it grew, it took on the characteristics of those who attended its birth and its nurturing. Its ancestors were European—creators of ballet from Italy, France, Scandinavia, Russia—but it came to take on the specific movement rhythms and accents and colorings of a new land. The creating of ballets on American themes was a part of the process of building an American ballet, but another part was the development of choreographers who instinctively incorporated American idioms into whatever they did and yet another part was the training of American dancers.

For performance was essential to the growth of American ballet, and the performing of ballet, though academically correct and meticulously respectful of established techniques, would have to reflect the speed, size, humor, expansiveness, bravado, energy, friendliness, athleticism of America. Without changing a step, Americans would dance *Les Sylphides* quite differently from the English, and other traditional ballets would find new colorings, new values when danced by Americans. This did not mean that Americans would be better dancers than those produced by other nations. It simply meant that ballet belonged to every nation and that every nation had the privilege and the duty of expanding its horizons. America answered the call.

14

The Regional Ballet Movement

The regional ballet movement is not only new in America; it is unique to it. Since the late 1920's there had been a trend in various communities to establish civic ballets. They were, and remain, nonprofessional companies made up of students from a local ballet school. For a period, while ballet interest was just beginning to expand in America, the local recitals by such groups served a "civic" function in that they showed parents, neighbors and friends how the dance students were progressing.

The late Anatole Chujoy, critic and publisher (*Dance News*), had been impressed with ballet festivals he had attended in Canada. Why not something of the sort in the United States, but organized on a yearly, nationwide, regionally oriented basis? He told his idea to Dorothy Alexander, who headed the oldest civic ballet in the United States (the Atlanta Civic Ballet, founded in 1929 as the Dorothy Alexander Concert Group), and the movement got under way with a festival (1955) involving five companies. So successful was it that in 1956 the Southeastern Regional Ballet Festival Association was formed. In 1958 the Northeast Regional Ballet Festival Association came into being; the third, the Southwestern, was established in 1963; and the fourth, the Pacific Western, in 1966. Five companies took part in the first festival in 1955; fifteen years later there were more than five times that number participating in the Southeastern region.

By 1971 there were close to one hundred regional ballet companies in the United States (and sprawling over into Ottawa, Canada), plus another two hundred or more unassociated civic ballets or local groups. The status of a regional ballet is that it belongs to one of the four regional ballet associations; it is incorporated as a nonprofit enterprise; it gives public performances for a paying public; it is nonprofessional, although it may have some dancers of professional caliber and call upon professional dancers as guest artists.

Some former regional ballet companies have been able to turn professional through money grants from foundations or government sources. Two examples would be the Boston Civic Ballet, headed by E. Virginia Williams, which received a Ford Foundation grant enabling Miss Williams to put key dancers on year-round salaries and to pay union scale for rehearsals and performances; and Barbara Weisberger's Wilkes-Barre student group, also with Ford Foundation aid, which shed its regional status, moved to Philadelphia and became the new Pennsylvania Ballet, drawing dancers from all over the state and from other sources as well.

The difference between a regional ballet company and a

professional one may be shown by taking two companies in Washington, D.C. The Washington Ballet, headed by Mary Day, is a first-rate regional ballet composed of students drawn from Miss Day's associated school and supplemented on occasion with a guest artist. The National Ballet (also centered in Washington) is headed by Frederic Franklin and is composed of professional dancers, some of them internationally known. The Franklin troupe performs not only in Washington but also throughout the United States and abroad.

The value of the regional ballet, through its association and annual festival, is that it emulates, to the degree it can, a professional troupe. Furthermore, at the festivals, local groups which might otherwise be isolated are exposed to what neighboring groups are doing. Styles and techniques, repertory and choreographic development are up for scrutiny at the festivals. There is rivalry, but teachers and pupils alike learn much from each other, be it through revelation or slightly jaundiced eye. Because of the regional ballet movement, the standards of ballet instruction, performance, taste and accomplishment have risen spectacularly throughout the American dance scene.

The regional-ballet movement has also spurred communities to give greater support to their local ballet company (or companies). Pride has been generated, and a ballet company which returns home after a successful appearance in a festival in a neighboring city or state is lionized almost as much as a sports team. The festivals, in turn, have inspired regional ballet companies to make little tours of their state or region, and these add a great deal to the prowess and polish of the young performers, mostly teenagers.

Participating companies and repertories for the annual festivals are selected not by the companies themselves and their directors but by outside ballet experts called adjudicators. These adjudicators have no associations with any companies or dance studios, and they perform their arduous services for expenses only. The adjudicator for a given region in a given year will travel to every city within that region which has a regional ballet and observe classes, rehearsals, run-throughs and performances. One national adjudicator, Alice Bingham, a former dance reviewer and assistant editor of a dance publication, has visited, on one tightly booked tour, twenty-two cities and made reports on as many as fifty ballets.

Each region may choose its own out-of-region adjudicator, but the choice is almost always made from a recommended list provided by the National Association for Regional Ballet, a sort of supercommittee composed of representatives from each region in addition to national dance celebrities with extensive dance experience as viewers of ballet, critics, editors and educators. Occasionally, a region will ask for an adjudicator who holds membership in a different region. For example, Robert Barnett, a director of the Atlanta Civic Ballet, could not adjudicate for the Southeastern Region, but he could, and has, for another region totally outside his own area of concern. The advantage here is to have as an adjudicator a person highly experienced in regional ballet activities but in no way prejudiced in favor of one or another group in a distant region.

Repertory for regional ballet companies adds the element of creativity, choreographically speaking, to ever-improving performing stature. Today, repertory for home consumption as well as for the highly competitive festivals includes much more than the old chestnuts of classical ballet. True, almost every company has its Christmastime *Nutcracker,* a ballet in which gilt-edged stocks should be made available, and it does its excerpts from *Swan Lake* or *Sleeping Beauty* or, perhaps, a complete *Les Sylphides,* but new ballets, some even with regional themes, are being choreographed by the director of the company, by a student who shows a leaning toward composition or even by a professional choreographer from the outside who brings in a successful ballet he has previously staged or designs a new one for a specific regional ballet.

Perhaps the most important aspect of regional ballet, in addition to elevating technical, performing and choreographic standards, is that it fosters decentralization in American ballet. From colonial times ballet was centered in only a few cities, and even after the nation had expanded from coast to coast, New York, Chicago and San Francisco were the key ballet centers, with New York in the lead by an immeasurable margin. New York City remains the dance capital not only of America but also of the world. However, regional ballets have brought acceptance of ballet, enthusiasm for ballet and even profound respect for ballet to the major communities of the United States.

A special dividend may well be the development of regional themes, of choreographies with roots not in big cities or even solely in the imaginations of city-oriented individuals, but in the lore, legends, music and mores of an area. Thus regional ballet can assist, beyond estimate, in the continued building of an American ballet representing the whole, not just part, of the land and its people.

15

Ballet from Abroad

Ballet in America, in the decades following World War II, comprised many things. The war itself, placing restrictions upon international travel, had permitted American ballet to sink its roots deeply into the soil, to build its own ballet stars, to foster its own choreographers, to convince a public in quest of relief from the pressures of war that ballet could be entertaining as well as artistically satisfying.

Following the war, the importations in all fields of dance commenced. The American companies were prepared to hold their own against the distinguished visitors from overseas, but American provincialism, the lurking doubt that art importations might be better than the home products, caused an imbalance from time to time.

In 1949 England's Sadler's Wells Ballet came to America for the first time. The response was tremendous. Individuals who had never attended ballet performances before rushed to get tickets to see the highly publicized company and were unbelieving when told that the American Ballet Theatre or the New York City Ballet were just as good, quite different, but coequal. Indeed, some of the national magazines, without a dance expert on the staff, were happily tempted to call the Sadler's Wells Ballet the greatest ballet in the world. This was ridiculous.

Equally exaggerated were the remarks on the other side of the question, such as "Take away Margot Fonteyn and *The Sleeping Beauty* and what have they got left?" In the first tour and the return visits, it became quite clear that the Sadler's Wells Ballet was one of the world's great companies. It was true that Fonteyn was its brightest star, a ballerina in the truest sense of the word, and it was also true that the full-length production of *The Sleeping Beauty* was a marvel of taste and beauty. But the company had many other virtues. It had the firm and disciplined direction of Dame Ninette de Valois, the contemporary choreography of Frederick Ashton and, although its male wing tended to be weak, some excellent principals and soloists.

In 1956 Queen Elizabeth II granted the company a Royal Charter and it became the Royal Ballet. In 1962 Ashton was knighted by the Queen, and in 1963 he succeeded Dame Ninette as director of the company, a post he held until he resigned in 1970 to devote full time to choreography.

In its first American seasons, the Royal Ballet made us familiar with and grateful for the virtually faultless dancing of Fonteyn, the bright and lively performing of Moira Shearer in the first engagements, the specialized gifts of Nadia Nerina and Rowena Jackson, the blossoming artistry of the lovely Svetlana Beriosova, the expert miming of

Pamela May, the strong and long-of-line qualities of Beryl Grey and some good male dancing by Michael Somes (an excellent partner and cavalier), Brian Shaw, David Blair and Philip Chatfield.

In later years Fonteyn continued to reign as the supreme ballerina. She found a new partner and co-star in Rudolf Nureyev, a brilliant Soviet dancer of the Kirov, who defected to the West in 1961 and joined the Royal Ballet the following year. Other important dancers have included Antoinette Sibley, Merle Park, Ann Jenner, Anthony Dowell and Alexander Grant.

With respect to repertory, the Royal Ballet has brought us not only *The Sleeping Beauty* but also such classics as *Le Lac des Cygnes* (*Swan Lake* in its full four-act form), *Giselle, Coppélia,* Ashton's new treatment of the program-long *Sylvia,* a rather lethargic *Les Sylphides* and a glittering *Firebird,* reproduced as close to the Fokine original as possible. In the modern ballet area, Ashton's works prevailed. There were his full-length *Cinderella,* which was not particularly well liked, and his zestful *Façade,* the hauntingly lovely *Daphnis and Chloë,* the elegant *Homage to the Queen* (the Coronation ballet), the non-narrative *Scènes de Ballet,* the comic *A Wedding Bouquet* and a large group of later creations, among them *Monotones Nos. I and II, The Dream, Marguerite and Armand, Ondine, Enigma Variations, Jazz Calendar* and other ballets, and Kenneth MacMillan's *Romeo and Juliet,* plus new productions of old classics and wholly new choreography (by Ashton) to the original score, edited, of the old *La Fille Mal Gardée* (1786). Nureyev restaged *Baya-*

dère (one act) and variations from *Raymonda* for the Royal dancers.

The visits of the Royal Ballet have enriched American ballet fare enormously. The performing style, which seems to stem from ballet's Romantic Age, is more lyrical than ours, less rhythmic organically but exceptionally musical with respect to phrasing, not especially dynamic, strong in mime but less concerned with the drama of action itself. Technically, of course, the standards are as high as any to be found. Differences lie in style, in approach, in stage deportment and, naturally, in choreographic inclinations.

A contributor to the dance landscape was the Paris Opéra Ballet, which made a brief trip to New York in 1948. It left, unfortunately, a not very happy impression. The New York City Center was not, admittedly, the ideal spot in which to see a company accustomed to a huge theater, elaborate stage facilities and an air of elegance which the City Center lacks completely. Still, one could find little cause for enthusiasm in this historic company, for much of the choreography seemed thin and feeble to our eyes, and although there were some striking individual performances, particularly that of Yvette Chauviré, the ensemble seemed careless, a group feeling appeared to be lacking and, surprising for a French unit, an unchic air characterized the stage behavior of certain of the dancers.

Representing the vitality and imaginativeness of France much, much better was the Ballets de Paris, headed by Roland Petit and featuring Renée Jeanmaire and Colette Marchand. The slick, modern troupe offered nothing traditional and, in a repertory which some felt was more closely allied to the musical-comedy stage than to ballet, gave accent to the drama inherent in dancing. The principal work was Petit's ballet version of *Carmen,* a highly sexy treatment of this passionate and melodramatic tale.

Dancers of the Royal Danish Ballet have brought yet a different style of ballet to the American theater. With a national dance tradition more than two hundred years old and a repertory which gave special place to the works of the nineteenth-century August Bournonville, the Danes have shown us a ballet form which gives particular accent to aerial actions, a bounding, darting view of ballet possessed of movement sequences quite different from (although the steps themselves were familiar) those composed by Russian, French, British or American choreographers. Because they are a classical ballet company, they have a *Swan Lake* and a *Coppélia* (in their own version) and the like, but they also boast the century-old Bournonville ballets, among them *Napoli* and *La Sylphide* (derived from Taglioni's first and greatest vehicle) as well as works incorporating Danish legends and folklore actions.

The Canadians also—the National Ballet of Canada, Les Grands Ballets Canadiens (which started out as a television dance group), the Royal Winnipeg Ballet—have brought their ballets across the world's friendliest frontier to remind us that the United States by no means has a monopoly on the New World's ballet. Rivalry is sharp, perhaps bitter, among them, yet they tend to complement each other effectively.

The National Ballet is especially concerned with the classics, with a standard repertory. An evening-long *Swan Lake* and a four-act *The Nutcracker* are in their repertory, as well as *Coppélia* and *Les Sylphides*. Contemporary works, however, do not find themselves neglected, for the company boasts productions of Tudor's *Lilac Garden, Dark Elegies,* and ballets by its director, Celia Franca.

The Royal Winnipeg Ballet, on the other hand, centers its interest in modern works, many of them on Canadian themes or created by Canadians. The company has grown into one of international stature and has earned ovations not only in the United States but also in Moscow, Paris and other world capitals.

All three companies receive annual grants from the Canadian Government to help pay for new ballets and to defray expenses.

In its American appearances, London's Festival Ballet disclosed a highly international flavor. With Anton Dolin as its director, the company was led by Tamara Toumanova (one of the original "baby ballerinas") and Nathalie Krassovska, both well known to American audiences, the French Violette Verdy and the English John Gilpin. And the repertory ranged from the old nineteenth-century *Esmeralda* through bits from Bournonville's *Napoli* to such standards as *Swan Lake* and *Scheherazade* and new works with new music. Under Dolin's expert and experienced supervision, everything was well disciplined, fast of pace and highly theatrical. Subsequently Gilpin, the troupe's premier danseur, became director. It is a company which features the classics in its repertory and guest artists in its personnel. Integrating Toumanova with anything is a nearly hopeless job, for she goes her own virtuosic way, dancing with incredible strength, overacting continuously and paying little if any heed to anyone else on stage or to the style of the company with which she happens to be appearing.

The Grand Ballet du Marquis de Cuevas, chartered in the United States by the Marquis as Ballet International in 1944, was always more European than American, since it performed only very occasionally in America. Rosella Hightower and Marjorie Tallchief, both Americans, were for some years its chief ballerinas. Bronislava Nijinska, Massine and George Skibine were among its choreographers. Nureyev, on his defection, danced with this company. The Marquis died in 1961, and his wife, the Marquesa, disbanded it the same year.

America got its first look at dancers of the Soviet Union (other than in movies) in 1958 when the Moiseyev Dance Company from Moscow made its first U.S. tour. It literally took the nation by storm—performances were sold out and ovations were standard procedure. The material was folk rather than ballet, but the dances from the various republics and regions of the Soviet Union were brilliantly theatricalized by the troupe's founder-director, Igor Moiseyev. Brilliant dancing, multicolored regional costumes, variety in both dance patterns and music provided the American public with a theatrical dance spectacle which it had never seen equaled.

In their first and subsequent trips to the United States, the Moiseyev dancers continued to attract vast audiences and to stimulate study of Russian, Byelorussian, Ukrainian and other folk forms in America's own folk-dance centers. Its enormous success also caused Americans to take a closer look at their own folklore in dance. Even the U.S. State Department queried dance experts on whether we could come up with an American equivalent of the Moiseyev. Agnes de Mille, America's foremost ballet choreographer on American folk materials, had already, before the coming of Moiseyev, made plans for an American dance theater rooted in our folklore. Only funds have been needed to bring it to fruition, and the amount was large since de Mille has insisted on careful research, conferences with folk-dance specialists, training programs and extensive rehearsal periods. The American Folk Ballet, headed by Burch Mann, has made a highly commendable effort to fill the void with her own theatricalized folk dances on American themes. The Moiseyev also succeeded in generating new interest in American folk themes for regular ballet repertory—de Mille's *The Wind in the Mountains* for the American Ballet Theatre would be an example.

The following year, 1959, came the long-awaited U.S. debut of the fabled Bolshoi Ballet from Moscow. This was the first time in history that Americans had seen on their own soil an official Russian ballet troupe (the Diaghilev company was a personal one made up of artists from the Imperial Ballet) either from Imperial Russia or the Soviet Union. The impact was immense. Curiosity drove thousands upon thousands to see the Bolshoi, but admiration called them back. The style was flamboyant, and Americans gasped at the one-arm lifts in which a stocky man hoisted a female at arm's length over his head or at the hurtles through space in which the male would catch the jet-propelled female at the last second. The Russian men were indeed heavy—they were compared to truck drivers—on this first tour, but the direction must have taken a tip from American ballet styles and in subsequent visits the males—a new group—were lithe and slender but still strong.

The almost legendary Galina Ulanova, who had been described as "the wonder of the world," danced for the first tour, although she was fifty, and won total praise for her performance of the teenage heroine in Leonid Lavrovsky's *Romeo and Juliet* (Prokofiev). Her movies had long since won the admiration of American balletomanes, but seeing her in person as Juliet and in *Giselle* marked experiences that all dance followers have continued to cherish. Another favorite was the blazing Maya Plisetskaya, as volatile as Ulanova was gentle. Her amazing leaps, her back kick in air in which her foot nearly touches her head, her flirtatious smile and her explosive personality have made her one of the world's most popular ballerinas, especially admired in America.

Like the Moiseyev, the Bolshoi made an instant impression on the American dance scene. Every American male dancer sought to emulate the prowess of the Russian male. Most of them tried the high lifts and found them not too difficult to do once the knack was discovered, and choreographers began to incorporate these feats of virtuosity—the hurtlings through space and the lifts—in their new works. "Bolshoi lift" became a part of the American dance vocabulary.

The Russian-American exposure worked both ways, for the Russians, seeing our ballet companies both in America and in their homeland, realized that they themselves were, choreographically, a half-century behind the times. Ulanova herself, loved, feared and respected, recommended the establishing of a ballet workshop in Moscow, and, after the first American visit, new choreographic advances were clearly discernible.

The Bolshoi's repertory has included the standard classics, *Swan Lake* and *Giselle* among them—plus the *Romeo*, *Bayaderka* (*Bayadère*) and many short pas de deux, show-off pieces, which are sure applause-getters in divertissement programs. Both Ulanova and Plisetskaya have captivated American audiences with their dancing of the old Pavlova-Fokine solo, *The Dying Swan*. Ulanova danced it with the subtlest of gesture, while Plisetskaya uses such sinuosity of the arms that one would think that she had been trained in East Indian dance.

After the Bolshoi Ballet came the Kirov Ballet (formerly the Ballet of the Maryinsky Theater) of Leningrad. The circusy aspects of the Bolshoi were missing and the accent was on the purest, most refined classicism. The two companies appear to be contemptuous of each other in Russia itself. It was interesting for Americans to see the Kirov since much of America's ballet style was rooted in the Maryinsky, which had produced Nijinsky, Karsavina, Pavlova, Balanchine, Danilova and many other stars. Among the stars especially admired were Alla Sizova and her husband, Yuri Soloviev, and Natalia Makarova, who defected to the West in 1970, as has been noted.

Carla Fracci, the first major Italian ballerina in almost fifty years, comes from La Scala in Milan, but she performs as guest artist in many countries. She has performed with the American Ballet Theatre and, with Erik Bruhn as her partner, is celebrated for her *Giselle* (which has been made into a feature-length movie starring Fracci, Bruhn, Toni Lander and Bruce Marks) and for *La Sylphide*. In the male category there is the Italian Paolo Bortoluzzi of Maurice Béjart's Ballet of the 20th Century—among the very few Italians to gain prominence in international ballet.

Other foreign visitors in the world of ballet who have played major engagements in America have included the Ballet Rambert; the Western Theatre Ballet, with a contemporary repertory, some of it treating controversial themes; the Netherlands Dance Theater, also with a contemporary repertory, but one in which both ballets in classical style and purely modern dance works are ingredients; the Polish Mime Theater, nonballetic but intensely theatrical and highly avant-garde in its use of gesture, free-style modern movements and fantasy; the Batsheva Dance Company from Israel, a modern dance group with works by Martha Graham, Anna Sokolow, Jerome Robbins, Norman Walker and young Israeli choreographers.

One of the world's great companies has been the Stuttgart Ballet, led by the directorial and choreographic genius of the British John Cranko and starring Marcia Haydée from Brazil and Richard Cragun from Sacramento, California. Cranko excels in evening-long ballets: *Romeo and Juliet, Eugene Onegin* and the rousing comedy ballet, *The Taming of the Shrew*.

Italy, which invented ballet, has been able to export nothing of balletic excellence except individuals in recent years, with Fracci as the supreme Italian dancer, but distant and young Australia has sent us its own Australian Ballet; and from little Belgium has come a company with an impressive name, Ballet of the 20th Century, with impressive young dancers (including non-Belgian dancers too, Americans among them) and headed by an impressive director, Maurice Béjart, whose choreography ranges from avant-garde creations through a *Swan Lake* with a male swan lead to Beethoven's Ninth Symphony!

Each American balletomane will have his own memory-image of dance and dancers from abroad. What would it be? For the older ones it might be the joyous steps of Alexandra Danilova and Frederic Franklin in the great waltz from *Gaîté Parisienne* or Massine as the funny Peruvian in the same ballet or Markova as a lighter-than-air spirit maiden in *Giselle;* it might be the girlish smile and the incredible balances on pointe of Dame Margot Fonteyn as Princess Aurora in *The Sleeping Beauty;* the animal grace, walking, leaping or waiting, of Nureyev; the elegance of Bruhn; Plisetskaya, shooting through space like a rocket; Sir Frederick Ashton and Sir Robert Helpmann as the clumsy Ugly Sisters in *Cinderella;* six Danish males bounding straight at the audience in *Napoli;* the masked, foolish diplomats brandishing their fists and preparing for war in Kurt Jooss's *The Green Table;* Jean Babilée, in sordid surroundings, hanging himself to the pure music of Bach in *Le Jeune Homme et la Mort;* the entrance, down a ramp, of a sequence of girls in white, moving from arabesque to arabesque until they fill the entire stage, in the Kirov's faultlessly danced *Bayaderka;* or the sentimental tribute, at New York's Metropolitan Opera House (1970), to Sir Frederick Ashton on the occasion of his retirement as director of the Royal Ballet, at which all the stars and all the corps of this huge company danced in excerpts from some of Sir Frederick's own works or from a favorite ballet.

Each will have his own image to cherish, but the nation as a whole will see how American theaters from coast to coast have played host to ballet and modern dance companies from around the world, and how what had started out as esoteric importations for the few has blossomed into a form of art and entertainment which has captured the interest, the enthusiasm and the devotion of millions of Americans.

16

Ethnic Dances

The bright and prideful dances of Spain, the physically graceful and spiritually profound symbolisms of India's classical dance, the movement poetry of Japan and many other forms of national dance arts have enriched our stages. They are not international forms, such as the classical ballet; not contemporary forms, such as modern dance; not the fruit of individual genius, although the individual may and does contribute to their vocabularies of action. These are ethnic dances created over the centuries or millennia by a race, by a people, and they are best divided into two parts, although the two frequently overlap: folk dances, which are designed primarily for participation, and ethnic dances, art dances built for performing by the highly gifted in theaters, in temples, in cabarets.

Certainly the first American artists of stature to recognize the inexhaustible heritage of ethnic dance were Ruth St. Denis and Ted Shawn. In their own individual programs and in those created for their Denishawn Dancers, these two presented theater pieces which derived from ethnic sources. To American audiences, they brought glimpses of Hopis and Aztecs, Hindus and Spaniards, the Balinese and the Siamese, modern North Africans, ancient Egyptians and many others. Sometimes they strove for ethnic accuracy, but more often they chose to use ethnic materials creatively in modern ballets with racial flavors, colors and idioms.

As dance in America commenced its twentieth-century ascent, the horizons of theatrical dancing began to spread even further than ballet, modern dance and forms popular in show business to include an ever-increasing amount of ethnic dance. At first, only the exotic natures, the strange surfaces of these art forms seemed to appeal to the public, and there were the doubting who believed that Americans would never catch on to the meanings of Hindu dance gesture or respond to the leisurely actions and alien themes of the Japanese classical dance. But persistently and consistently, ethnic dance forms have penetrated the American theater, and so thoroughly that extended seasons and long tours by dance troupes and soloists from Spain, India, Japan, the Philippines, nearby Mexico and distant Africa are possible. And ethnic dance, sometimes adapted but occasionally pretty accurately reproduced, has even found successful outlets in musical comedy, opera ballet and night-club shows.

The principal figure in America's fostering of ethnic dance has been La Meri (a Texan girl named Russell Meriwether Hughes), an unusually versatile dancer equipped by intensive training and natural gifts to capture the movement styles, techniques and, strangely enough, even the facial characteristics of many races. In her performances, as a soloist or with full company, she has presented dances from India, Spain (these two nations in particular), Bali, Siam, Burma, Java, Japan, China, Hawaii, the Philippines, North Africa, Cuba, Mexico, Peru, Ecuador and yet other lands.

In almost every case she has recreated with exactness these dances of many lands, and in her New York academy, the Ethnologic Dance Center (1942–1956), she sought not only to pass on to students the movement techniques of various ethnologic dance forms but also to share her vast knowledge of the histories, cultures, religious concepts, philosophies and customs of those peoples whose dance arts she has brought to Americans.

By way of proving the universality of dance and its common eloquence, she has used the classical movements and gestures of Hindu dance to retell the story and reproduce the choreographic form of *Swan Lake,* a notable and fascinating achievement. Furthermore, she has taken the gesture language of the Hindu dance to communicate the meanings and moods of non-Indian songs, among them the great Christian hymn "Holy, Holy, Holy," the Jewish "Eli, Eli," the Negro spiritual "The Creation" and a collection of popular songs.

That La Meri concentrated upon the dance of India and Spanish dancing was not mere happenstance, for it is inarguable that these two countries have produced the most varied, most complex, most virtuosic and, to our eyes at least, the most theatrically stirring schools of ethnic dance. Interestingly enough, the two distant nations have an ancient dance alliance, for through traveling gypsies, originating in India, something of the rhythms, a touch of gestural pattern were carried across the centuries and across intermediate lands to Spain.

La Meri, retired from the New York scene, continues to teach ethnic dance to amateurs and to produce ethnic dance festivals by professionals in the popular resort area of Cape Cod. In her seventies, La Meri could look back comfortably and happily, knowing she had contributed more than any other American to the making of a friendly climate for dance importations, ethnic dance created by other peoples, other cultures.

During America's dance renaissance in this century, one of the first great Spanish artists to visit our shores was the late La Argentina, a dancer of enormous personality and high artistry. Her first appearances were far from successful, but suddenly, in 1928, a series of New York concerts captured the interest of press and public and La Argentina became, as far as Americans were concerned, Spanish dance.

Although she had been born in Argentina, Spain was her artistic motherland and for Spain she accomplished a notable service. For it was due, to great extent, to La Argentina's careful researches, theatrical power and consummate artistry that Spanish dance could move on from cafés, cabarets and revues to the concert stage, there to find recognition (or rerecognition) as a superior dance art form.

The next great female Spanish dancer of importance to triumph in America was Argentinita. Like her senior, she also had been born in Argentina but grew up in Spain and made her first successful appearances there. Yet another similarity was that her American debut, in a revue, was an unhappy affair. But Argentinita returned as a concert dancer in 1938, and from then until her death in 1945 she remained the Spanish dance favorite of the American public.

A mistress of the many schools and styles of Spanish dance, Argentinita was equally at home in the gracious classics, the fiery gypsy dances or the bouncing jotas. She was not only a superb technician but also a highly accomplished actress and singer, and her comic skills—delicate but sharply etched—enlivened several of her dance vignettes. One of her most appealing numbers was, peculiarly enough, not Spanish. It was *Huayno,* an Inca Indian dance from Peru, which was simple of step but so wistful and tender that she and her sister, Pilar Lopez, who danced it with her, invariably had to repeat it.

Of the top Spanish male dancers, one of the first and greatest to appear on the contemporary American dance scene was Vicente Escudero. He, too, was a scholar as well as an artist, and it was his special desire to restore Spanish gypsy dancing to its purest forms and to bring to the stage new examples of old and long-hidden gypsy-dance characteristics.

Small and lithe, this virtuoso was famed for the clarity of his brilliant footwork and for using his fingernails—either playing them against each other as a clicking accompaniment or using them to rap out rhythms on a wooden chair seat—in addition to finger-snappings, the striking of palms and castanets, as a method of self-accompaniment.

In the 1930's Escudero attained his greatest popularity in America, but he returned to Spain and sank into relative obscurity. In the mid-1950's this man who had been acclaimed the greatest Spanish male dancer in generations came back to America as an old gentleman prepared to make his farewell to audiences who had loved him and to those younger ones who knew only his legend. Slower of movement and not quite as erect as he once had been, Escudero nevertheless recaptured his public with the dignity and perfection of his dancing and with a delicious humor that had come to replace some of the old-time fire.

Among Escudero's successors, some of the principal ones are Antonio, the American-born José Greco, José Molina, Ciro, Antonio Gades, Roberto Ximenez and Manolo Vargas, Maria Alba, Rosario Galán and many more as interest in Spanish dance has grown. Each, in his own way, has extended the delight in Spanish dance for many Americans. Antonio and his former partner, Rosario, were known as the Kids from Seville, and their youthful, athletic and fiery representations of Spanish gypsy dancing earned them ardent admirers on the night-club circuit and, later, in the concert field. After their separation, Antonio formed his own Spanish ballet company and augmented his area of Spanish dance to include non-gypsy numbers, among them some splendid regional dance forms. With increasing maturity and undiminished technical skill, Antonio has risen to become one of the top Spanish dancers of the day, loved in his native land and enthusiastically admired in America and other countries.

On the distaff side, the Spanish dance also boasted the dynamic, explosive Carmen Amaya, a gypsy whose heel-beats sounded like the rattle of machine guns, whose finger-snappings were like bursting balloons and whose swiftness of action sent combs and roses flying through space and brought a stunning blur to the onlooker's eye. Amaya, who died in 1963, was, however, an artist through and through, for with fire were perfection of form, controlled passion and enormous dignity.

Carola Goya, a veteran in the field of Spanish dance, is an American who has succeeded in mastering an alien art. Perennially youthful, she was particularly handsome in classical dances, and her playing of the castanets represented one of her major accomplishments. In retirement, she turned to teaching and coaching and assisting her younger ethnic dance associate, Matteo (a pupil of La Meri).

Ruth St. Denis created ballets, solos and duets based upon the themes and styles of Hindu dance, and Anna Pavlova included the dance art of India in her programs, but it was Uday Shankar, who had aided Pavlova in her excursions into Oriental dance, who not only led the dance in India through its twentieth-century renaissance but also gave Americans their first look at authoritative, beautifully produced and artistically elevated authentic Hindu dance. Shankar was highly creative, but his sources were deep in the soil of Indian tradition and his schooling was exact in all technical matters. With his first American visit in 1931, he introduced audiences to the surface colors and exoticisms, the profound themes, the complex movements of Hindu dance. Few understood the complicated gesture language, but its abstract beauties were sufficient to fascinate most. With subsequent tours, the visits of other dancers from India, the pioneering work of La Meri and the publication of literature on the forms and substance of Hindu dance, Shankar's powers were increasingly appreciated and the dance of India came to be an accepted part of the American dance scene.

Another of India's great dancers, Ram Gopal, has also

toured America, exemplifying quite a different style of Indian dance from that employed by Shankar. Shivaram, Priyagopal, Shanta Rao, Balasaraswati and that brilliant male virtuoso, Bhaskar, and many of their countrymen and countrywomen have journeyed to the United States to offer their particular Hindu dance specialties. But Indians are not the sole representatives of the dances of the East. Many years ago, Mei Lan-Fang, China's foremost actor-dancer, brought his art to America, and, in recent years, with China isolated from many countries, its very special dance arts have been demonstrated and taught by Sophia Delza, an American modern dancer who received intensive training in Chinese action dances in China itself.

The Japanese dance has had many important individual exponents, among them Yeichi Nimura and Sahomi Tachibana, but America saw its first large-scale Japanese dance theater in 1954 when the Azuma Kabuki Dancers and Musicians made their New York debut. The company did not pretend to offer the pure Kabuki repertory, but it did, in that season and in the following year, offer examples of Kabuki dance art performed by genuine Kabuki artists in addition to regional dances and contemporary theatrical dance choreographies. More leisurely of pace than Hindu dance, Japanese dancing, however, avoided the barrier established by the symbolic gesture language of Hindu dance. Its themes and characters were strange to Western eyes—perhaps no stranger than Shiva or Radha or the Monkey God of India—but few had any trouble in pursuing the dramatic line or responding to incident in the Kabuki's repertory.

Later, Gagaku, the Imperial Household Musicians and

Dancers of Japan, performed here, and a classical Kabuki troupe also visited America. Among the results was a new ballet, *Bugaku,* choreographed by George Balanchine to a score commissioned of a contemporary Japanese composer for the New York City Ballet. It combined classical Western ballet technique with Eastern dance gesture.

The Dancers and Musicians from Bali also arrived, to present a still different form of Eastern dance. Here there were complex gestures, but, unlike the hand symbols of Hindu dance, they were more decorative than meaningful. The pace of action was faster, the music of the gamelan, though highly exotic, seemed less strange to the West than accompaniments from India or Japan.

The facets of Oriental dance in America, however, were far more numerous than those supplied by the big companies and the great stars. Mara brought to America the dances of Cambodia; Devi Dja and later arrivals gave representation to the dance of Java; and from Sumatra, Hawaii, Korea, Iran and other nations and other regions came still more performers to make large or modest contributions to America's expanding theater for Oriental dance.

For many years, the lusty strength, ceremonial splendor and many styles of African dance were seen mainly through travel films; then Asadata Dafora came from West Africa to stage for New Yorkers the dance dramas of his people, and Pearl Primus went out from America to the land of her distant ancestors to rediscover and recreate the dances of Western and Central Africa. Before this, the flavors of African dance were by no means unknown to Americans. United States citizens of African descent had long incorporated steps and rhythms from the old lands into new forms of American dance.

The debt that the dance art of the New World owes to the onetime African is incalculable, but while African rhythms were being absorbed into the dances of the Western Hemisphere, the pure African dance was neglected. At first, Dafora stirred American audiences with the striking qualities of pure African dance. Next, Primus, with modern-dance training and considerable knowledge of West Indian dances, traveled to Africa to study, master and transplant (or adapt) the current tribal dances to the American theater.

African dance rites of many kinds, some lustily primitive, others almost gentle in their near-Orientalisms, still others (as in the dances of the Watusis) as elegant as the ballet, and all mirroring a vast dance culture, were included in the Primus repertories. Ultimately, Primus sought to give balance as well as range to her work and set about the building of a series of dance programs which would show African dances, West Indian dances of African derivation, American dances with colors from the old continent and contemporary dances on contemporary themes of concern to the Negro and to the American.

Dance companies have been springing up in the newly independent countries of Africa. The first—and one of the best—to visit America was Les Ballets Africains from the Republic of Guinea. Here tribal dances and ceremonies had been shrewdly edited and theatricalized and performed by dancers and musicians selected by contests and auditions in the villages of Guinea. Other African countries have followed similar procedures in building theater-dance companies from folk materials.

Some folk dances, because of their vitality and intricacy of step, are occasionally theatrical in their original shapes. This is especially true of the dances of many of the various ethnic groups in the Soviet Union and of Balkan dances in general. The Moiseyev Dance Company, using regional dances from the Soviet Union, has not only taken the best of the steps and the patterns, but has theatricalized them. Furthermore, the ballet training of the dancers provides them with extra prowess. Other troupes—the exuberant Ukrainians, the booted-toe-dancing Georgians, the colorful Macedonians, Poles, Yugoslavs, Rumanians—have all fused folk authenticities with shrewd theatricalism for export.

Not all of these Balkan dances are theatrically effective. Some are participation dances which would be far more exciting to do than to see, but others—and this is true of the men's dances—call upon the rhythmic abilities of individuals, and thus dances which have to do with battle, with contest or with simply showing off make the transfer from village gathering to stage easily and effectively.

Amalia Hernandez, founder-director-choreographer of the Ballet Folklorico de Mexico, travels from village to village, selecting the best steps for a given dance and molding them into a tight, expert synthesis of the dance. By studying glyphs, sculptures, architecture and ancient codices, she has reconstructed in theater a pre-Columbian past. Other choreographers in other cultures pursue a similar course of authenticity and creativity.

217

As for the world's folk dances, almost all of them enjoy survival, growth and expansion not only in their native habitats but also in America. Because of the numberless racial strains which make up the complexion of the nation, folk dances from other lands are immediately understandable. Old World customs are happily recalled not only through special dishes and costumes carefully saved but in the constantly reborn measures of dance. Across the country, folk-dance groups enjoy not only America's own square dancing and those folk dances which long back came from other lands and adapted themselves to the New World but also recent importations from England, Ireland, Scotland, France, Poland, the Ukraine, Germany, Sweden and almost any other nation one cares to name. In New York alone it is possible to find folk-dance sessions and classes devoted to dances from many lands which provide nostalgic reminders to new Americans and new rhythmic adventures to old-time citizens.

And where on the ethnic-dance scene does the American Indian, who represents America's purest native dancer, find his place? His dances, of course, live on in his tribal ceremonies, but as the white man's culture encroaches upon the ancient ways, there is the ever-present danger that, one by one, the dances will be forgotten or retain only their shells for tourist interest. Efforts, however, are constantly being made to preserve the great and highly varied dance cultures of the various Indian tribes. Annual festivals in the Southwest, in the Plains, the Woodlands and elsewhere, while attracting tourist trade, help to keep alive the age-old ceremonials.

In other areas folklorists and the Indians themselves have

initiated projects—festivals, intertribal celebrations, the recreation of old Indian villages and the manner of living—whereby arts and crafts may be encouraged.

Theatrically, Indian dances were limited for many years to Wild West shows, circuses, carnivals and Western movies. Recently, however, attempts have been made to bring Indian dances to the stage in terms of art. Two who have served the cause of Indian dance most effectively are non-Indians, Reginald and Gladys Laubin. The Laubins have lived with the Plains Indians, studied their tongue, shared their games and labors, investigated their lore and, from some of the old men of the tribes, have learned dances and ceremonies which were on the verge of disappearing.

To the theater, they have brought the substances as well as the authentic forms of Plains Indian (and certain other) dances, for they have not only mastered steps but also learned the reasons—spiritual, playful, philosophical—which motivate the dances. Through their pioneering, they have introduced audiences, both in America and abroad, to the very genuine dance art of the American Indian, demonstrating that shouts, war whoops and stampings are but a minor aspect of a dance art rich in movement subtleties and virtuosities. Not the least of their contributions is the enthusiasm for Indian dance that they have generated in the Indians themselves, rekindling the memories of the old and stirring the young to a new pride in their great heritage.

Of dancing Indians, one of the best known is Tom Two Arrows, an Onondaga Indian of the Iroquois Nation, who has successfully brought the dance of the Eastern Woodlands Indians to the stage, lecture platforms and television. Reversing the trend of importing ethnic-dance forms to America, Tom Two Arrows has traveled to the Orient, where he has demonstrated to the Indians of India the dance art of the Red Indian of the New World.

The purity of ethnic-dance forms is to be cherished, but there is no reason why such dances cannot lend their flavors to other theatrical activities. The ballet has long used national dances in adapted measures for its productions. Spanish, Russian and Italian folk measures have found their way into ballets, and modern dancers have used the characteristics, if not the actual steps, of ethnologic or regional folk dances by way of establishing scene or heritage. In Martha Graham's *Ardent Song,* for example, Oriental qualities of motion and design are present although the movements themselves are built upon pure modern-dance concepts, and in Doris Humphrey's *Ritmo Jondo,* created for José Limón and his company, the rhythms of Spain are suggested in the footwork and the characteristics of the Spaniard are reflected in the strong, proud bearing of the body, yet this, too, is a modern-dance work.

In her great ballet, *Rodeo,* Agnes de Mille has incorporated American folk-dance measures and the nondance movement characteristics of the cowboy with the actions of ballet, and in many of her Broadway shows she has displayed her mastery of a choreographic form combining the brilliance of ballet with the warmth and sweetness of the folk dance. In *Annie Get Your Gun* Helen Tamiris fused modern dance with steps characteristic of the American Indian to create a stunning ballet, and in *The King and I* Jerome Robbins translated the story of *Uncle Tom's Cabin* into *The Small*

House of Uncle Thomas, an irresistible ballet which spoke through the delicate and aristocratic terminology of Siamese dance.

In *Magdalena* Jack Cole caught the movement styles of Ecuadorian Indians for his dances in that musical, and in his *Kismet* the whirling dervishes of the East found a Broadway home.

These and other choreographers of musicals, movies, ballet and modern dance have found that ethnic dance is a source of movement riches, that it need not be employed in its purest forms but that it can give color, flavor and special identity to highly creative, contemporary works.

17

Musicals, Movies, Television

Dancing has always had its place in that wing of the theater devoted to outright entertainment. Of course, some great artists took part in vaudeville shows and musicals, but they were there because they were stars, because they had gained renown in their own special fields of endeavor. Vaudeville appearances by Ruth St. Denis, Martha Graham or Anna Pavlova were exactly like those made by, say, Sarah Bernhardt. No one lowered or changed her artistic standards; rather did each bring her special art to the so-called popular theater. For the rest, musicals and vaudeville relied heavily on hoofers, eccentric dancers and a line of girls who could kick in unison and look fetching.

For many years, dancers had a "turn" on stage. They were there to give a change of pace to a show and, if they happened to be stars, to have a show built around them. But they were rarely used in their dancing capacities as integral figures in the carrying out of the plot. No, dancing was a specialty; it was not, in such times, a very special means of emotional, dramatic and narrational communication.

The popular theater, naturally, had its own dance stars, genuine artists. The 1920's boasted Fred and Adele Astaire, Marilyn Miller, Harriet Hoctor, to name but a few. They were stellar performers, attractive personalities, splendid dancers. Through such as these dance had a place of honor in musicals and vaudeville. But dancing itself had yet to serve a given show in full eloquence, projecting tragedy, mirroring passion, advancing the plot line.

There were exceptions. Doris Humphrey and Charles Weidman, in the early 1930's, brought their new brand of art dance to the musical-comedy theater. Then there was ballet's George Balanchine, who caused a minor artistic revolution with *On Your Toes,* a musical with a ballet background and a magnificent number called "Slaughter on Tenth Avenue." And there was Robert Alton, associated with a number of popular Broadway hits, who decided that since dancers could dance they should be given an opportunity to do so. Using popular dance forms, jazz and Latin-American rhythms, Alton did something about the old-style line patterns. He did away with most of them—except where they were pertinent—and substituted imaginative designs, intricate movements and actions which had meaning as well as rhythm.

With Agnes de Mille's dances for *Oklahoma!* in 1943, the whole concept of musical-comedy dancing was forever changed. De Mille used ballet, modern dance, folk dance, dramatic gesture. She also used artist-dancers. But, more than all of these, she made dancing a living part—not just a "turn"—of the musical itself. Her now-famous dream sequence from the show was proof enough that dancing could say things that no words could convey and say them in terms that a nondance audience could understand. Her dances were not rhythmic exercises, not tricks, not mere diversions. They spoke for the hearts of lovers, they revealed terrifying and wonderful secrets, they identified the characteristics of a people.

De Mille was neither the first nor the last to bring this concept of dance to the nondance theater. Perhaps Hoctor had a feeling for this concept when she danced her solo, "Ma Belle," in *The Three Musketeers,* and after *Oklahoma!* had become history, Esther Junger used the powerful symbolism of dance in a drama, *Dear Judas,* to herald the coming anguish of the Crucifixion long before the betrayal occurred. But de Mille was the first to make this application of dance stick to the ribs of the musical theater.

With de Mille's success, it was inevitable that other great choreographers would be engaged to bring their dance powers and sensitivities to the new musical comedy, already emerging as a lyric theater. Jerome Robbins, Helen Tamiris and Hanya Holm earned new acclaim outside their fields of ballet and modern dance. Michael Kidd, Jack Cole, Valerie Bettis, Anna Sokolow, Donald Saddler, Bob Fosse and others came to join them and de Mille in the Broadway theater.

Times had certainly changed. Robbins' ballet *Fancy Free* was extended into the hit musical *On the Town,* which he, of course, choreographed. *High Button Shoes, Billion Dollar Baby, The King and I* and other hit musicals followed as this young American master of choreography flooded his talents into Broadway projects as well as into ballet, movies and television. In Tamiris' *Inside U.S.A.* Bettis had danced, to storms of applause, a pure modern-dance solo, the exact sort of work which either she or Tamiris would have felt to be of concert-dance caliber.

In *Brigadoon* de Mille included a long solo dance of lamentation, and in her famed *Carousel* she let dance reveal in visions what was in the heart, what dialogue could not possibly express. The eloquent dance of the deaf-mute in Kidd's *Finian's Rainbow* was yet another example of a new truth, that the American public was at last willing to accept dancing not merely as a diversion but as a method of revelation, a means of communication.

With *West Side Story* Robbins achieved total theater, for acting moved into dance and back imperceptibly, just as speech spilled from sentences to poems to song. This modern treatment of the Romeo and Juliet theme was classical in concept, a renewal of the theater of ancient Greece. With *Fiddler on the Roof* Robbins made use of Jewish dance rhythms, as Saddler did with *Milk and Honey*, a show about the new Israel.

Gower Champion, long popular as a show-business dancer with his wife Marge as partner, has become pre-eminent as choreographer-director for musicals. Onna White, Ronald Field, Joe Layton are among others who have contributed to the expanding accomplishments of the American musical.

The stirring success of dance in musical comedy did not mean that lightness and joy and fun were replaced with message-laden dances. Popular Latin-American rhythms were danced with high abandon, spoofs on the twenties brought back the Charleston, jitterbugging (a real American folk form), the twist and its descendants, rock music and dance gave their energies and physical virtuosities to the scene, and tap dancers and pretty chorus girls also had their moments of glory. A balance, indeed, had been found, for just as a musical had place and need for a lovely ballad as well as for a hot tune, so it needed a dance which ranged from the breezy, rhythmic marvels of the tap dancer to the haunting beauties of a dream sequence, a dance of lamentation or the silent speech of a mute who could find communication only in the moving muscles of a feeling body.

Were the line dancers, the tricksters, the strutting show girls gone forever from the scene? Certainly not, for they would have been sorely missed. There were those who used the technical tricks of the ballet upon which to build a specialty, such as a spinner, a jumper or a back-bender. One could find acrobatic dancers, contortionists and such novel activities as a dancer playing the violin while doing ballet turns (not so new when one realizes that French dancers in colonial times attempted the same feats, sometimes even using a tightrope as part of the act).

Line dancers, in fact, achieved a new glory at the Radio City Music Hall in New York. For it is here that the thirty-six Rockettes move with faultless precision throughout their colorful and imaginative routines, tap-dancing their way to a finale which includes a few measures of unison kicking as they line up across the front of the great stage. Under Russell Markert's direction, the Rockettes have become almost a national institution, and only the most narrow-minded dance devotee would fail to place them among the most delightful of America's dance attractions.

The Music Hall also has its resident corps de ballet, usually numbering thirty-two dancers, and its service in familiarizing movie-going audiences, in pre-television days, with ballet cannot be overestimated. Again, the narrow-minded could say that the Music Hall's ballet was far from subtle. It was not intended to be, for it was there to abet the cause of spectacle. With Florence Rogge as its long-time director (she was succeeded by Margaret Sande, Marc Platt and others), the corps appeared in shortened (timewise) but enlarged (physically) versions of a number of classics, such as *Swan Lake, Les Sylphides* and *Coppélia,* as well as danced original ballets by Miss Rogge.

Crowded with people and jammed with tables as they customarily are, night clubs on occasion find room for dancers as well as for singers and comedians. One such spot, for example, was New York's Latin Quarter, which once had pretty show girls who could do little more than walk to music, as well as a tap-dance headliner or an exhibition-ballroom team or a dancer with an unusual act. Occasionally, some of the leading figures of concert dance and ballet would do a night-club stint. Tamiris, Weidman, Argentinita and others all performed in such spots, and so also did the ballet's high-flying Paul Haakon, who seemed to soar over the tables in his search for dancing space.

The movies, attracted to dance, have tried almost everything and everybody. Sometimes the medium has turned out some highly distinguished dance work, but often it botches the job. Usually it is at its strongest when its star is a dancer, not simply a stage artist but a genuine movie star (albeit with a stage background) such as Fred Astaire, Ray Bolger or

Gene Kelly. For in the Astaire or Kelly films dancing has been not merely a decorative incidental, which could be deleted or cut or otherwise tampered with, but the main ingredient, the star's material.

The long line of Astaire films brought superlative dancing to millions of movie-goers around the world. His swiftly tapping feet discovered hundreds of joyous patterns, indoors, out of doors, over furniture, everywhere. He could make a lullaby to a girl by doing a soft shoe on a sanded floor over her room or he could spin her happily along pathways, wooing her in wooded glades. Perhaps the girl was one of his most famous co-stars, Ginger Rogers, or perhaps another, but whoever it was, he danced with her and for her, spoke to her with his dancing and, on occasion, talked to himself through his dance. For Fred Astaire made dancing a perfectly natural expression of joy, and in his fine films, dialogue and dance, pantomime and dance, courtship and dance, playfulness and dance were firmly interwoven.

That motion-picture dancing has progressed as far as it has is due, in no small measure, to the efforts of Gene Kelly. For Kelly was not only a first-rate tap dancer and a skillful choreographer; he was also a willing and imaginative experimentalist. Although he was unquestionably the star of his motion pictures and the center of dance interest, he saw to it that his own dancing was supported and extended by the dancing of others, sometimes soloists, sometimes groups of dancers. He knew, obviously, that movies could create fantasy and aspects of spectacle better than any other medium and he did not hesitate to explore the possibilities. Not content with simply photographing dances, he used the camera's inherent mobility and almost magical perceptiveness to seek out dance details or, through absolutely appropriate fantasy, make the dancer a part of the wind, the rain, the sky, just as the dancer really is in his own dreams.

Other distinctive dance skills have contributed immeasurably to the development of motion-picture dance since the days of the early sound pictures when dance interludes were based mainly upon hordes of pretty girls arranged in geometric patterns or upon the individual dancing of such solo experts as Eleanor Powell or George Murphy or Ruby Keeler. Balanchine came along with classical ballet materials and with a new view of the camera's possibilities. Still later, Cole, de Mille, Kidd, Robbins, Roland Petit, Bettis, Holm, Rod Alexander, Loring and others extended cinematic dance still further with the aid of an array of performers ranging from Vera Zorina, successful in ballet and musical comedy, to Leslie Caron, Cyd Charisse, Gene Nelson, Donald O'Connor, Shirley MacLaine and Bobby Van.

With *Seven Brides for Seven Brothers,* produced in the mid-1950's, the movies fully exploited what Broadway had known for a decade: that dancing could be a part of the plot itself, a perfectly natural medium for the delineation of character, the evoking of mood, the heightening of incident. Michael Kidd was the choreographer, and twelve—six boys and six girls—of the fourteen principal figures indicated by the title were dancers. And they danced.

There were several striking formal dances arranged by Kidd—a big, roaring barn dance and a tender dance for the brides—but what was especially noteworthy was that in one scene six of the brothers interspersed measures of moody, dreamy dance with their labors of chopping, sawing and piling wood. Dance here was used to communicate the word-less thoughts of their minds, their feelings as they went about humble farm duties. The roaring fight between the brothers and the boys of the town was an out-and-out fight, but it was choreographed nonetheless, for it had form and pacing and design.

With the advent of television, dance had the home-visiting opportunities denied it by radio. At first, only the lightest kind of dancing was considered suitable for audiences pre-sumably composed of those with a minimum of dance ex-perience. However, there were first-rate experimental shows involving such choreographic pioneers as Pauline Koner and Paul Godkin. Unfortunately, these initial programs were not popular. Perhaps the dancing was to blame, perhaps the formats of the shows themselves were awkward, perhaps the TV public was not ready for anything but simple enter-tainment.

Producers and sponsors, frightened by the failure of these initial dance-flavored shows, put dancing on a blacklist for several years. As the medium commenced to expand broadly, however, dance returned, this time to triumph. Choreog-raphers and dancers who had been earning small weekly salaries (when they worked) suddenly found themselves in the four-figure-per-week category for their choreographic duties on television. Young and unstarred dancers found new sources of income through television as show after show added permanent dance troupes to its complement of per-formers.

James Starbuck, John Butler, Rod Alexander and Tony

Charmoli have been among the most successful over a long period of time, and then came Ernest Flatt, the late Carol Haney, Wallace Seibert, Hugh Lambert, Danny Daniels, Peter Gennaro, Ron Fletcher (who also does ice shows), Walter Nicks, Donald McKayle, Kevin Carlisle. Duties ranged from staging musical numbers to giving dance form to popular songs. Starbuck and Alexander once had particular success in working with the so-called "Spectaculars" (later called "Specials"), involving dance stars, a huge corps and opulent production numbers. Butler, although he has long worked with popular materials, has tended to experiment in the art shows for television where he has had opportunity to work with unusual or highly classical musical scores, adult themes, fantasy.

Personal imagination and a thorough understanding of the limitations and potentialities of the TV screen have been required of choreographers for the successful use of dance in the new medium. A large company, except when carefully used, tends to be ineffective, for the figures are reduced to unidentifiable midgets on the screen. Flatness, in a medium which is by nature two-dimensional, also has to be avoided and certain movements which are exciting on stage become negative when screened. Thus the choreographer needs to be something of a technician, a director, if dance is to emerge with its intrinsic values unimpaired.

Charmoli, in his long years with "Your Hit Parade," employed a small number of dancers and frequently used them moving from a distance into or away from the camera, thus creating a sense of depth as opposed to the flatness which could come from dancers spread out horizontally across the camera's face. Naturally, camera tricks were not all that he used, for his dances, though brief and allied with hit tunes, were representative of distinguished choreography.

As to the dance themes and forms used by TV, it can be said that nothing is skirted. There are tap dances, ballets, geometric figurations, visualizations of popular songs, acrobatics, specialties, folk dancing, many ethnologic dances, children's pieces, fairy tales, avant-garde experiments and, of course, social-dance forms ranging from gavottes and galliards through the ballroom dances of the twentieth century, among them the dances made famous by Vernon and Irene Castle, the later Charleston, black bottom, big apple, rumba, samba, mambo, the twist, the frug and rock.

Guest artists have included almost everyone of any stature from the theater of dance: St. Denis, Shawn, Markova, Danilova, Tallchief, Hayden, Eglevsky, Jeanmaire, Slavenska, Limón, de Mille, and more recently Fonteyn, Nureyev, Bruhn and even whole companies such as the American Ballet Theatre, the Royal Ballet, the José Limón company, the John Butler Dance Theater, the Greco group, the Moiseyev Dance Company and those others who have made names for themselves on the stage.

The success of dance and dancers on TV, following its early stumbles, is now a fact. Hardly a show of a variety or musical format can get along without choreographers and dancers. And in the prestige productions dance either plays a leading part or takes over entirely. When Mary Martin's celebrated *Peter Pan* was arranged for television, Jerome Robbins, who had choreographed the theater production, staged the TV version (1954), including the dances themselves, the musical numbers and Martin's own spectacular flights on wires.

The industry was surprised and almost shocked at the popular response to a ninety-minute program devoted entirely to the Sadler's Wells Ballet (now the Royal Ballet) production of *The Sleeping Beauty* (1955) with Fonteyn starred. The producers were panicky enough to insert an idiotic playlet which explained to the viewers what the ballet was about, but this negative bit failed to destroy the presentation itself and organizations which compile viewer ratings discovered that some thirty million persons sat happily watching this televised ballet. Dancing on television had come of age.

The unexpected (by the television powers) popularity of *The Sleeping Beauty* gave new courage to those who guide the destiny of the television business. Plans for other ballets were immediately announced; de Mille went on with a strikingly planned and wholly adult forty-minute lecture demonstration on the evolution of the ballet. The Royal Ballet did a full-length *Cinderella*. The National Ballet of Canada also did a *Cinderella,* which won a TV Emmy Award (1970). "Camera 3" produced a series of dance events, including lecture-demonstrations, classical ballet, avant-garde works and even technique-anatomy classes. And suddenly it became apparent that dance was not for special interests but for everyone. The theater had discovered this truth much earlier, and now the television industry was prepared not only to accept this fact but also to bring dance the largest audience it had ever had in the history of the art.

18

Dance Education and Recreation

Dance in education? Of course it belongs. But to some who might, with justification, be called "old codgers," the pre-Duncan, pre-St. Denis view of dance prevails. And there are those who defiantly proclaim that they had no dance lessons when they went to school and that they emerged with a good education. Quite true, but neither did they nor their fore-bears have electronics or atomic energy or other subjects that man has added to his ever-growing list of conquests and discoveries.

Indeed, until a few years ago, the theater at the Jacob's Pillow Dance Festival and school directed by Ted Shawn was classified by the township of Becket, Massachusetts, as a "dance hall" (and was taxed by the township accordingly!). The federal government and the Commonwealth of Massachusetts recognized the Jacob's Pillow dance center as a nonprofit educational institution. Not so Becket. But there are Beckets and their equivalents all over the nation, and dance has managed to survive and to grow as an educational force.

Dance first entered the public schools as a recreational activity. Its form was the folk dance, and one of the prime forces in its move into the field of education was America's most famous folk-dance authority, Elizabeth Burchenal.

For more than fifty years, folk dancing has been considered a fine recreational study in the American public-school system, a study usually reserved for girls and almost always included in the schools' physical-education programs. Almost all physical-education instructors were required to take some courses in folk dancing, and even the elementary teachers were supposed to know something about the subject for use with their young charges.

But although folk dancing has fulfilled its duties perfectly, folk dancing is not enough. Dance has other qualities to offer the general student. The dance form which has prevailed in the educational field is modern dance. Some ask why the ballet was once excluded. The answer is simple. Ballet requires the mastery of an academic vocabulary of movement before the individual can even start to dance. The average college student, carrying a load of courses, did not, it was thought, have sufficient time in which to gain a working command of this special vocabulary. With modern dance, the beginner experiences dance with his first rhythmic steps. The ultimate virtuosic range of both ways of dance is the same, and as dance curricula in the colleges expanded in the 1950's and '60's, more ballet courses were introduced. By 1970 universities not only had their modern-dance groups but also dancers trained in ballet. The first major ballet department in college was founded in 1951 by Willam Christensen at the University of Utah. Today this university sponsors modern dance, ballet, folk dance, dancing for children in the community, theater and opera dance.

And just what can dance do for the student who has no intention of becoming a dancer? Physically it can strengthen the body, correct (in most cases) faults, develop coordination, enhance accuracy of movement and, because dance is a science of movement, provide a more thorough physical education to the student than calisthenics normally can.

Emotionally, dance aids students in adjusting themselves to group activity, to leadership, to discipline, and it helps them in matters of personal poise, in articulation, in the expression of ideas. For dance is both a discipline and a release. It demands a controlled body and, in group dances or in any kind of choreography, it requires the individuals to follow the rules. But it also invites the student to say what he has to say in terms of form and movement, to "dance out" his feelings, to discover his fellows while moving through the patterns of dance.

It is obvious that the mind, as well as the body and the emotions, is called into use, for the mind itself must become alert, disciplined, facile, if it is to command the body to move in ordered forms and if it is to translate ideas and sensations into dance, into compositions that are as clear to the viewer as to the doer.

In many and extensive surveys of dance in education, it has been discovered that dance in the colleges is customarily offered in the department of physical education, that an increasing number of colleges are offering dance as a major study resulting in a degree in dance, that in certain institutions dance has been transferred to the department of fine arts, that modern dance remains the favored technique, that the demand for dance instructors with a college degree is often greater than the supply and that dance is now pretty generally considered to be an important element in higher education.

The surveys showed that dance standards varied from college to college. In some, only elementary modern-dance technique was offered; in others, a broader technical base and some composition were listed; while in a few, several grades of technique, composition, music for dance, dance history and criticism, teaching methods, dance notation (usually the dance script known as Labanotation), kinesiology, anatomy, percussion, production and workshop experience constituted the dance program.

In many institutions of higher learning, dance was a course for girls only, although the men were occasionally permitted to take classes and engage in workshop activities without academic credit. Elsewhere, dance was equally available to both men and women.

Discrepancies in the standards have long haunted the profession of educational dance, but improvements are constantly, if slowly, being made. The trouble about men students is, of course, a hangover from the days when dancing was considered mainly a feminine activity. In certain colleges men students have rhythmic gymnastics but not dance, but often this is simply a method to soothe old-time convention, for in the majority of cases modern dance is taught, only the title is altered.

Arguments for male dance in education are exactly the same as those voiced for the female. Athletic coaches have been known to recommend dance training as an aid to the sports player; others have felt that dance was for those aesthetically inclined. Both, of course, are right. Dance serves many needs, among them that overused but still important word "integration." It is the province of dance to integrate body, mind and emotions into unified, ordered action. It does just that. As to the masculinity of dance, it may be said quite simply that dance is neither masculine nor feminine until either a male or female starts to dance. When a woman sings, the art of song is given feminine expression, tonality, quality; and when a man sings, the male equivalents of the voice are in command. The same holds true for the human body. Lecture demonstrations, conducted by stars such as Villella and by dedicated teachers, have done much to bring boys of a community to dance and to win approval for dancing for men.

In the country's elementary and secondary schools dancing (both folk and modern and occasionally some ballroom dance) is recommended if not always offered. In one survey it was discovered that commissioners of education in every state in the union endorsed the use of dance in the public-school systems of their states. Because of local conditions, financial, sometimes religious, or often because instructors could not be obtained, these recommendations are not always implemented. But in many of the big cities dance plays an active part in public-school curricula.

But again, the boys are unfairly treated educationally, for in a goodly number of the public schools both boys and girls get dance games and rhythms during the elementary grades, but in the secondary grades the boys are forced to drop out while the girls continue their dance experiences. Why boys are eliminated arbitrarily remains a mystery, but any change (even if it is for the general good) in any public-school setup is, if not actually suspect, endlessly delayed.

Innovations, however, are not unknown to our public schools. Among New York City's many vocational high schools is the unique School of the Performing Arts, where the students, taking a regular academic course, specialize in the arts of their choice. Among these performing arts is the art of dance. Directed and taught by a good-sized faculty of dance experts, all of them experienced in performing and not individuals whose background has been limited to collegiate dance, the boys and girls study both modern dance and ballet, along with ethnic forms, character dance, history and criticism.

The success of the dance department of the School of the Performing Arts is attested to by the numbers of graduates (and even undergraduates who are free during vacation periods) who have moved from the school directly into jobs with ballet companies, modern dance groups, musical shows and television. Among the former students who have achieved fame are Edward Villella, Arthur Mitchell, Bruce Marks, Norman Walker, Eliot Feld, Brunilda Ruiz, Eartha Kitt, Pat Crowley, Lee Becker Theodore.

Educational dance has come a long way—from nothing to an important if not adequately standardized aspect of education—in a few short years. Two of its greatest guides and fighters have been Margaret H'Doubler, until recently the director of dance at the University of Wisconsin, and Martha Hill, for years director of dance at Bennington College and New York University and later head of the dance department of the Juilliard School. From these two pioneers came the first teachers to go out and extend modern dance as an educational force into other colleges, and from them came concepts, schedules, programs and curricula suitable to the growth of dance education. First under H'Doubler and later under Hill (who at one time studied with the senior teacher), dance became a major course of study at their respective institutions, and before many years had passed, a doctor's degree in dance was possible.

H'Doubler and Hill, naturally, did not accomplish their great task alone. The cooperation of physical-education departments helped the cause beyond measure, and lesser-known dance educators did their own pioneering quietly and determinedly in their own states, regions and universities. The artists also took part in the effort, taking time off from performing duties to bring their vast dance learning to the new field.

The chief dance-festival and dance-education centers have been the Jacob's Pillow Dance Festival and its associated University of the Dance near Lee, Massachusetts; the Bennington Festival and school at Bennington, Vermont; the Connecticut College (New London) School of the Dance and the American Dance Festival (the Connecticut College summer sessions were continuations, with much the same personnel, of the Bennington seasons); the Perry-Mansfield School of Dance and Theater at Steamboat Springs, Colorado, all summertime dance centers where students and

teachers went for intensive training and where festival programs, featuring new creations, were given.

But not all dance education takes place in the public and
private schools across the land, in colleges and universities, in
academies (such as the Juilliard School) or in summertime
festival centers. The greatest area of instruction (it is a safer
word to use here than "education") is to be found in the
thousands of private dance schools which dot the country
from coast to coast.

Here, in these dance schools, there is no standardization
whatsoever. A teenage girl can teach faulty and dangerous
ballet methods in a poorly lit, unventilated basement; at the
same time there are great studios with enrollments in the
hundreds, where some of the world's finest teachers instruct
children and beginners, intermediate and advanced pupils,
boys and girls, nonprofessionals and the most noted stars of
the dance in the techniques of the art of dancing.

Off and on over the years, there has been sporadic talk of
licensing dance schools in various states which have no controls at all. But usually teacher groups fight against licensing.
Some teachers may have reason to fear that their standards
are so low that they would never be granted a license, others
may feel that interference of any sort is undesirable, and still
others may question who in a state government is equipped
to establish dance standards of teaching and what inspectors
are sufficiently schooled in dance to pass judgment on a given
school.

In the main, responsible teachers have preferred to work
together in dance organizations for the betterment of their
own profession. Not all such groups actually do what they set

out to do, but in certain cases conventions and master classes and lectures expose the membership's weakest teachers to new ideas, better teaching methods and the like. The regional ballet movement has, of course, done more than any licensing could do to raise teaching standards across the nation.

Sadly, the growing interest in ballet has tempted teachers of dance with little ballet experience to offer ballet classes, but a skilled tap-dance or ballroom-dance instructor is not necessarily a good ballet teacher. There have been inferior ballet teachers in the past, but there are more than ever now and they constitute a real threat. Sometimes they permit a child to wear toe slippers much too soon (eager mothers must share the blame in this), not realizing that toe slippers should not be used until the child is about twelve years old and then only after two years of solid and careful groundwork in the technique of ballet itself.

Dance education and dance instruction cover vast areas of the country and include every dance way known to man (it is possible, for example, to learn Maori or Inca Indian dances in New York). The most popular form is, of course, ballroom dancing, although with the 1960's and its twist, frug and descendants, and the unstudied motor response to rock music, formal ballroom class enrollments, except for pre-teenage children, fell off precipitously. But for years the international Arthur Murray studios meant "dance" to the average man.

Modern dance also has its studios in every major city, and its popularity may be indicated through the work of one teacher, Steffi Nossen, who has more than one thousand students in New York's Westchester County alone, where she and her staff teach grade-school and high-school students under the auspices of parent groups, although the classes themselves are not included in the schools' curricula.

How many dance schools of all kinds are there in the United States? Only estimates can be made. Massachusetts, in a careful tally, has more than one thousand dance schools of all kinds, some numbering only a handful of pupils, others with enrollments in the hundreds. At least two million new students a year enter classes in some form of theatrical dancing, mainly ballet, and the number of those receiving ballroom-dance instruction over short or extended periods of time is beyond computation.

In addition to the educational and recreational uses of dance, the art has its therapeutic aspects. Dance as therapy for the physically injured or mentally ill has long since proved its worth. It has aided paralytics to walk, to move their fingers, to straighten their spines, to achieve muscular controls where such controls were badly impaired.

In many institutions for the mentally ill, dance is used not only for recreational ends but also as treatment. Because the rhythms of dance exert considerable power over the emotions, and because dance is an activity which calls upon the integrated effort of body, mind and emotions, its value in helping to restore balance to the unbalanced is recognized and used. Dance cures, especially for those suffering from temporary shock (often these are soldiers), are by no means unknown. Experts, of course, are essential to the proper use of dance as therapy. Occasionally, the dance instructor is trained in psychology or, more often, in anatomy. Usually, the dance instructor in such cases works under the direction of the patient's physician.

But the therapeutic attributes of dance are always present, even when therapy itself is not the specific goal. Little children, in their dance games, find themselves and each other as they move in rhythm, master simple patterns, express their ideas, report and dream, imitate the wonders of nature they see about them or reveal fear, humor, love. For dancing is natural to man; he needs it (despite the restrictions imposed by civilization and custom), and it is good for him.

19

Dance Notation—Archives

The ephemeral nature of dance makes every method of re-
cording its fleeting wonders a precious instrument. Words,
symbols, films: these are the major methods of recording the
action of dance. Drawings, sculpture, photographs: these are
the major methods of recording movement pause, be it a
quiet pose or the peak of a leap.

From the wall paintings of the ancient Egyptians through
the fanciful lithographs of the Romantic Age's ballerinas,
pictures of one sort or another have provided clues to the
dance dress of an era, to dance themes, to style and, sometimes, to actual movements. Without such pictures, it would
be impossible to attempt to recreate, either literally for stage
purposes or in our minds, images of bygone dances.

Sometimes, skillful drawings of a dancer in action seem to
provide better records than photographs. Certainly, the superb action sketches which Abraham Walkowitz made of

Isadora Duncan constitute one of the most valuable records of the movement genius of that great woman.

And then there are words. Symbols they are, but universal ones which invite images of thought and action. Our finest records of ballet during its initial centuries of growth are to be found in the writings of professionals or of individuals who attended ballet performances; in rare books on dancing; or in programs which listed the names of performers and perhaps provided synopses of ballet and opera-ballet plots.

Anton Dolin, in recreating the famous *Pas de Quatre* which Taglioni, Grisi, Grahn and Cerito danced for Queen Victoria at a command performance in 1845, used ballet reviews of the day to guide him in patterning special material for each of the ballerina figures.

Today, America has a goodly number of dance critics, dance reporters and general reporters setting down their impressions of dance performances in newspapers, periodicals and books. Actually, there are not nearly enough dance critics in the nation to cover the vast amount of dance activity which takes place throughout the land. A few newspapers have dance critics, many newspapers rely on pinch-hitting music critics, and, in small cities, reporters and even sportswriters are called in to record and comment on a dance event. Special dance publications provide the enthusiast with intensive dance coverage.

Dance books, of course, give the reader far more dance details than reviews and columns in newspapers and magazines can do. Newspaper criticisms, naturally, are often compiled for book publication, but they are expanded, supplemented by additional descriptive materials. The literature, if that is not too pretentious a word, of dance has provided the art with a highly satisfactory and often distinguished, if incomplete, method of recording. The paucity of dance writing which characterized our past has been replaced by the quantity of dance-book publication in the period commencing with the mid-1930's and particularly since the end of World War II.

But if writing helps to record a dance performance or the specific style of a dance artist or a given choreography, it cannot do the job completely, for personal memories and impressions, likes and dislikes are involved. This is fine, for critical opinion is of undeniable importance in upholding standards of excellence, in placing a dance or dancer in perspective with respect to the contemporary dance scene and dance history.

Exactness in recording dance can be supplied by two methods: motion pictures for the recording of actual performance, and notation (a dance script) for recording choreography. Films are to dance what phonograph records are to music, and Labanotation (the most successful of dance scripts) is to dance what scores are to music. A less complex and increasingly popular notation system is that copyrighted in 1955 by Rudolf Benesh and his wife Joan. It is the official system of Britain's Royal Ballet and is favored in much of Western Europe. Where Labanotation uses a vertical staff, suggesting an upright body, Benesh uses the horizontal staff familiar to musicians. The recorder in the Laban method is called a notator; in Benesh, a choreologist.

Movies and video-tape recordings are of inestimable value in preserving primitive dances, ethnic dances which are on the point of disappearing or subject to adaptations. Ritual dances which can never be recreated on the stage, ceremonials in which the frenetic force of nonprofessional worshipers through dance is inseparable from sacred surroundings can be recorded on film.

The great performers of the theater can hope for performing permanence only through motion pictures. Notation will save their dances, but only movies can hope to capture their personalized dance gifts. How fortunate we are to have fragments of Pavlova's dancing on film. They are sketchy, not well made, and Pavlova herself never considered them to be anything more than experiments, but to us they reveal glimpses of her legendary magic and help to transform fable into fact.

As far as anyone knows, Isadora Duncan never made any movies, experimental or otherwise, and so she must live through words, drawings, photographs. But her great contemporary, Ruth St. Denis, has been preserved on film. There are movies of her at the peak of the Denishawn days, but even more important are the color movies made of her in later years, films which record almost all of *Radha* (a successful experimental film made by Dwight Godwin), *White Jade,* *The Nautches,* fragments of *Salome,* four historic solos (*White Jade, The Cobras, The Yogi, Dance of the Black and Gold Sari*) filmed by Marcus Blechman and produced by William Skipper, and a documentary of her life, spanning ninety years.

For dance purposes, perhaps the most valuable films are those made by amateurs or by professionals working on low budgets with a minimum of production facilities and equipment. These are rarely great movies as movies go, but they concentrate upon the performing artistries of individuals in key roles. Godwin, Ann Barzel (the Chicago dance critic), Thomas Bouchard and Walter Strate are among those who have attempted to preserve the dancing of great dancers and their dances or favored roles. There are also highly professional short films of Martha Graham and her company, starting with *The Dancer's World*, a documentary of Graham's approach to technique and choreography, and continuing with films of her great works (*Appalachian Spring, Night Journey,* etc.).

Hollywood has also made dance short subjects, but the producers have generally been more concerned with production, with translating a stage work to the screen (a perfectly valid method and often more desirable than simply recording a stage piece), than with giving immortality to special artists of dance. Highly imaginative film experts, such as the late Maya Deren, have made wonderful use of cinematic dance. But here, in this chapter, we are not concerned with the many fine achievements of professional film companies, in Hollywood, New York and abroad, which have used dance materials in the making of essentially cinematic works of art or entertainment but, rather, with film as a method of recording performance.

However, if movies are essential to the recording of individual performances, they are not altogether satisfactory in recording choreography. If a given ballet or solo dance had to be restored through film records, the style of a company, the idiosyncrasies of the individual performers, the highly developed personalities of the stars would, obviously, color the choreography and the resultant restaging of the work. The cold accuracy of notation is far the better method in such instances.

Systems for notating dance action, just as musical sounds are notated by scores, have been invented, tested, used for a time and supplanted for more than four hundred years. Names were given to steps and positions of the body, and for a time these were sufficient to enable anyone who knew the names to recreate a dance. But as theatrical dancing became more complex, diagrams showing floor patterns were employed, and eventually a system was devised in which stick figures, representing dance steps, moved along the lines of a musical staff.

These and other methods, as dance increased its scope, became either inadequate or so complicated that they were of little use. Individual choreographers have (and still do) worked out personal shorthand schemes which help them remember their own works, but, basically, dance needed a notational system which could serve every form of dance known and be prepared to serve all coming innovations. The systems which have done this job successfully are the one invented by the famous German dance pioneer Rudolf von Laban and improved over the years since its beginnings in 1928 by Laban and his European and American associates, and the Benesh method.

Labanotation, as the system is now called, has its American headquarters in New York City at the Dance Notation Bureau, established by Ann Hutchinson. Working closely with Laban and other experts in the dance-notation field, Hutchinson helped to perfect the method and to encourage not only its acceptance but its use. Through her efforts and those of her colleagues, courses in Labanotation have been introduced in dance schools and colleges; choreographers for ballet, modern dance and musical shows have engaged experts from the bureau to record their works; and, most recently, publication of notated dances has been achieved.

The system itself is most authoritatively and clearly described in the Hutchinson book *Labanotation* (New Directions, 1954), but, briefly, it may be said that its symbols, placed on a vertical staff (instead of the horizontal staff used for music), can notate every movement of the body from a leap to the flutter of a finger, direction, rhythm, intensity, design, the relationship of one dancer to another in a group plan, levels of action and, indeed, every choreographic essential.

The accuracy of Labanotation has been checked and rechecked countless times in student workshop groups and also on professional, theatrical levels. It works without error. So at last, through Labanotation, choreography need nevermore be lost or half-forgotten or altered through the passage of time and the faulty memory of man. How much of the original *Giselle* remains in the productions we see today, no one really knows, but we may be certain that many of the most important contemporary ballets can be restaged fifty years from now with exactness, with untampered choreography. Benesh, easier to master, has proved invaluable to the recording of dance in an age of prolific creativity.

But if Labanotation and Benesh are equipped to serve the future, they also had immediate practical applications. Choreographers and dancers dealing with large and changing repertories forget quickly, and often a work which has been at rest for a season or so needs more than the choreographer's memory to get it back into shape again. If the work has been notated, restoration is a simple process. Not every choreographer or dancer reads notation, but more and more are learning it, and meanwhile notational experts are always available to transcribe symbols back into movement.

The history of dance as preserved by films, symbols, art objects and memorabilia also needs a home. The home can be in private collections, in museums and in libraries, but dance archives, however they are cared for, are essential to the choreographer, the composer, the designer, the dancer, the student, the researcher.

There are dance archives in most of the capitals of Europe, some of them privately administered and others parts of national theater collections. America is also commencing to build up its dance archives. The Harvard College Theater Collection has long housed valuable dance items; for a time, the Museum of Modern Art in New York had a dance-archives section, and there were impressive individual collections such as those amassed by George Chaffee, Walter Toscanini, Lillian Moore (the foremost historian on American dance), Ruth St. Denis and Ted Shawn (with their Denishawn collection) and other individuals, many of them dancers.

Some of the private collections have now been made available to the public, and one of the newest centers, and also one of the best, for dance research in America is to be found at the New York Public Library in its new Museum and Library of the Performing Arts at Lincoln Center. For many years the library's music library provided the dance researcher with some of his best materials and it continues to serve, but in 1947 the central building in the old headquarters at Fifth Avenue and Forty-second Street commenced to build its dance collection under the direction of its first dance curator, Genevieve Oswald.

Under Miss Oswald's supervision of the library's dance division the library has received several of the important individual collections: the Denishawn materials (containing over thirty thousand items), the Cia Fornaroli Toscanini collection, the Humphrey-Weidman collection and innumerable gifts from other collectors. It is now believed to be the largest dance archives in the world. In addition to its own original items—a vast collection—it has microfilms of materials in dance collections from all over the world. In 1970 the Dance Collection, under Miss Oswald, inaugurated a computerized cataloguing system which would make available instant dance facts to the student-researcher.

All of the items have their importance. The rare lithographs capture with delightful fantasy dance images from the past, and the yellowing newspaper clippings have the magical power of giving a sense of immediacy to a dance event long forgotten. For the fleeting art of dancing, such a repository of dance materials not only symbolizes a monument to past achievements but also serves as a guide, as a source of inspiration to future creativity.

Other American cities have their dance collections, some large and others small, and these, together with the dance archives of the New York Public Library, provide America's swiftly increasing dance population (both doers and viewers) with opportunities to study the rare riches of the dance past.

20

In Conclusion

As the eye searches the vast dance landscape of America, still other figures come into view, figures which do not conform to ballet, modern, ethnic schools; others which never dance but contribute to dance; some with highly specialized dance services to offer.

Laughter is an important part of the American heritage, and laughing at oneself is a particularly cleansing quality. Most choreographers and dancers treat with humor at one time or another, but a few make fun their business. Iva Kitchell was one of these. It was her purpose (and our joy) to poke pertinent but friendly fun at classical ballet, at modern dance, at ethnic forms, at scarf dancers and operatic bacchantes.

As she went in search of her soul (à la Martha Graham), or gave pained exaggeration to the ballerina's technical tricks, became hopelessly tangled in veils and garlands, munched grapes and raced around with ewers in a scene which could be connected with the opera *Samson and Delilah,* reproduced the weary kicks of a bored showgirl or knocked to pieces a Spanish dance, Kitchell pricked merrily at the weak spots or potentially funny spots of the finest forms of dance and made us love her and dancing even more.

Mata and Hari have carried buffoonery and satire into teamwork as they have reproduced an entire symphony orchestra and its movement activities or amused themselves with the solemn ceremonial of Hindu fakirs. With Lotte Goslar and the great French mime, Marcel Marceau, satire is present but the heart-touching sadness of the ridiculous clown gives quite different color to their danced humors.

In Angna Enters the art of dance mime found its most celebrated exponent. For although Enters included in her huge repertory many numbers which were entirely pantomimic, her most powerful characterizations were built upon or threaded with the action of dance. These would certainly include the lascivious *Boy Cardinal,* with the roving eye and surreptitiously played castanets; the haughty dancer of *Pavana,* with the promise of murder-to-come in her glance and in the angry shudder of a shoulder; *Moyen Age,* with its intense report of the miracle of the Annunciation; *Queen of Heaven,* a gestural blessing of incredible beauty; the hilarious *Balletomane-Connoisseur;* the sex-heavy *Odalisque;* the glittering *Byzantine Ikon.*

Americans of this generation have been notoriously uneasy in mime, not in conveying the drama of dance (in which, perhaps, they excel), but in formal mime. The weakest sections in our productions of traditional ballets are those which require a command of the art of mime. Outside the ballet,

Enters carried mime to a new peak in her highly personalized creations, and the American Mime Theater, directed by Paul Curtis, has attempted to build a repertory of mimed ballets, American in flavor, which will exploit that area lying between straight pantomime and dance proper. Mime, however, has not been a forte with American dancers, although they have learned to do it well within the framework of classical ballet.

The desire to explore the unexplored has accounted for many of America's most impressive dance achievements, a fact amply proved by the careers of Duncan, St. Denis, the leaders of modern dance and others. But exploration must and does continue.

Other special figures have crossed the dance landscape. In the early years of the century there was Maude Allan, who almost made a career out of her dance interpretation of *Salome*. Much later, there was Tilly Losch, skilled in both ballet and modern dance, famed for her exotic roles and perhaps best remembered for her dances which stressed the fluidity and expressiveness of her hands.

The late Bill Robinson was an imposing and beloved figure on this scene and so also was Pegleg Bates, who transformed a handicap into a special virtuosity, and there are those whose many talents lead them into so many enterprises that they never can be categorized, those such as the beautiful Vera Zorina, who has moved from ballet to musical comedies to movies to acting to symphonic narrations.

New to the dance scene are opera ballets of which the dance profession need not be ashamed. In the past, of course, opera ballet had its moments of stirring experimentation and it occasionally drew choreographers, such as Balanchine, and attractive soloists, such as Ruthanna Boris, Lillian Moore, Felia Doubrovska, Maria Gambarelli, Marina Svetlova and others, into its fold. But in the main, opera ballet remained stagnant, found itself relegated to a subminor post and was regarded with lightness or contempt by the independent dance theater.

By the middle of this century opera ballet commenced to stir. Zachary Solov, a young choreographer and dancer, was engaged by the Metropolitan Opera to stage its ballets, and from the first it was clear that his fresh ideas would invigorate and expand an old, old form of dancing. With the aid and encouragement of the Metropolitan's director, Rudolf Bing, Solov came up with several lively and distinctive ballets and dance interludes for the operas, among them *Aïda,* in which he succeeded in flavoring an Italianate work with archaic Egyptian movement designs; *Orfeo ed Eurydice,* for which he obtained the services of Alicia Markova as ballerina; *Manon,* brief and simple but delightful in its evocation of a period; *Die Fledermaus,* with its waltzes; *Samson and Delilah,* with its bacchanale. Since Solov's day at the Met, ballet highlights have rarely emerged, and the old routine of unobtrusive opera ballet has prevailed.

Our dance scene also includes those who represent the sister arts, for although each art possesses independence, collaborations among them bear fruits of great beauty. Music scores have been born through a union with dance. Adolphe Adam's music for *Giselle,* Delibes' scores for *Coppélia* and *Sylvia* and Tchaikovsky's music for three great ballet classics (*Swan Lake, The Sleeping Beauty, The Nutcracker*) have long been loved for themselves as well as for their services to dance.

The list of those composers who have shared their gifts with ballet, modern dance and even dances for musicals is tremendous. Just a portion of that list is awesome: Stravinsky, Hindemith, Bernstein, Copland, Barber, Chavez, Menotti, Schuman, Antheil, Dello Joio, Poulenc, Haieff, Gould, Thomson, all of them represented in dance works familiar to American audiences and contained in American dance repertories.

Painters and designers are a part of the collaborative plan. When the Diaghilev ballet first came out of Russia, the scenery and costumes designed by such artists as Bakst, Benois and Gontcharova shared in the dancers' triumphs. Later collaborations brought to the dance theater the artistries of Rouault, Picasso, Matisse, Derain, Chagall, Dali, Tchelitcheff, Berman, Bérard, Colt, Beaton, Robert Rauschenberg, Marisol and Larry Rivers, the sculptor Isamu Noguchi and such first-rank stage designers as Jo Mielziner and Oliver Smith.

Art assistance of still another sort has been given to dance by experts in lighting. Of these, the most distinguished was the late Jean Rosenthal, who designed the lighting for the New York City Ballet, Martha Graham and her company and other theatrical groups. Rosenthal used lighting not merely to define the bodies of the dancers as they moved in space or to bathe the scenery in pleasant lights, but also choreographically, demanding that it contribute to the establishment of mood, that it seek out the constantly shifting centers of movement interest, that it enhance as well as reveal, that its own patterns complement the patterns of dance.

So successfully did Rosenthal apply her lighting methods to the needs of dance that she often made scenery and formal costumes seem unnecessary. She did full justice, of course, to the beauties of a Chagall setting or to the always fabulous costumes of the matchless Karinska, but she could also dress the dancers' stage with the colors of her lights and give almost architectural dimensions to that space through which the dancers moved. Thomas Skelton, Jennifer Tipton, Nicholas Cernovich, Alwin Nikolais and Lar Lubovitch (a lighting expert as well as a fine dancer-choreographer) are others who have made the art of lighting an integral part of the art of dancing.

As one looks at America's dance landscape, the horizon seems to reach infinity, potential frontiers seem endless and the dancing figures to be without number. Each image has its importance. It may be the exciting image of Martha Graham, as a leg soars high toward a zenith of ecstasy, or it may be a motionless and very modest pile of magazines called *Dance Index,* which served the art of dance briefly but brilliantly. It may be the shimmering image of a Tallchief skimming on impeccable pointes across the range of vision or it could be the silent, watching critics—Carl Van Vechten, John Martin, Mary Watkins, Margaret Lloyd, Edwin Denby, Anatole Chujoy, Louis Horst and the others—who strove to record the elusive images of dance.

It is a landscape which belongs equally to Ruth St. Denis, who danced across it for seventy years, and to the unbeliev-

ably beautiful Takako Asakawa (of the Graham Company),
dancing brightly toward the summit of her ambitions, to the
masterful choreographic patterns of a Balanchine and to the
refreshing choreographic searchings of a Feld, Smuin, Lubovitch, Falco, Arpino, Taylor, Cunningham. For the world-
renowned, the well-known, the promising, the unknown and
the striving are all here on this landscape, each a contributor
in his own way to the dance in America, each an ardent
believer in that great vision proclaimed by Isadora Duncan:
"I see America dancing."

Index

Index

Charisse, Cyd, 229
Charleston, 225, 232
Charmoli, Tony, 230–232
Chase, Lucia, 178, 179
Chatfield, Philip, 196
Chauviré, Yvette, 197
Chavez, Carlos, 258
Chinese dance, 214
Choreartium, 169–170
Christensen, Harold, 186–187
Christensen, Lew, 174, 175, 186, 187
Christensen, Willam, 186, 187, 236
Christian church and dance, 16
Christy Minstrels, 34
Chujoy, Anatole, 189, 259
Church of the Divine Dance (Hollywood), 64
Cia Fornaroli Toscanini Collection, N.Y. Public Library, 253
Cinderella (Ashton), 196, 205, 233
Cinderella (Franca), 233
Ciocca, Giovanna, 33
Circe, 94
Circular Descent, 105, 107, 108
Ciro, 213
City Center Joffrey Ballet, 155, 161, 184; *see also* Joffrey Ballet
Clair de Lune, 89
Clifford, John, 177
clog dances, 28, 35, 157
Clowns, 184
Clytemnestra, 94–95
Cobras, The, 59–60, 65, 248
Cole, Jack, 221, 224, 229
Coles, Hony, 159
Collins, Janet, 160, 162
Color Harmony, 105, 107
Color Study of the Madonna, 66
Colorado College, 121, 128
Colt, Alvin, 258
Columbia Artists, 171
Columbus, Christopher, 16
commedia dell' arte, 16, 25
Con Amore, 186
Concerto Barocco, 175
"Conflict," 134
Connecticut College School of Dance, 240
Conrad, Karen, 178, 179
"Constitution Hornpipe," 35
Coon Town, 158
Copland, Aaron, 258
Coppélia, 166, 186, 196, 198, 227, 257
Coralli, Jean, 31
couple dances, 4
courtship dances, 4; of animals and birds, 13
Cragun, Richard, 204
Cranko, John, 204
"Creation, The," 209

critics and criticism, 246–247
Critique of Pure Reason (Kant), 54
Crowley, Pat, 239
Cunningham, Merce, 147, 148–149, 150, 151, 176, 260
Curtis, Paul, 256
Cycle of Unrest, 134

Daddy Rice, 34, 157
Dafora, Asadata, 215, 216
Dalcroze, Émile Jaques, 121
Dalcroze School (Dresden), 122
Dalcroze School (Frankfurt-am-Main), 122
Dali, Salvador, 258
Daly, Augustin, 40
d'Amboise, Jacques, 177
dance, 3–13; primitive, 13–14; in colonial America, 23–29; in 19th century America, 31–35
Dance Congress (Munich), 123
Dance Index, 259
Dance Moods, 132
Dance News, 189
Dance Notation Bureau, N.Y., 250
Dance of the Ages (film), 73
Dance of the Black and Gold Sari, 248
Dance of the City, 133
"Dance of Day, The," 61
Dance of Introduction, 128
Dance of Life, The (Ellis), 3
"Dance of Night, The," 61
Dance of Work and Play, 128
Dance Repertory Theater, 134
dance schools, 241–243
Dance Theatre of Harlem, 163
Dance Theatre Workshop, 151
Dancers and Musicians from Bali, 215
Dancers Studio, 146
Dancer's World, A, 249
Dancing (Dodworth), 36
Danielian, Leon, 172, 179
Daniels, Danny, 231
Danilova, Alexandra, 169, 170, 171, 172, 203, 205, 232
Danse, La (Genée), 166
d'Antuono, Eleanor, 183
Daphnis and Chloë, 196
Dark Elegies, 181
Dark Meadow, 94–95, 97–98
Dauberval, Jean, 181
David, King of Israel, 15
David and Goliath, 118
Davis, Sammy, Jr, 159
Day, Mary, 191
Day on Earth, 8, 108, 110
Dear Judas, 224
Deaths and Entrances, 94, 163
de Basil, Colonel Wassily, 22, 169, 170
de Cuevas, Marquesa, 200

Index

Index

Index

INDEX

About the Author

WALTER TERRY was born in New York City and brought up in New Canaan, Connecticut. He first studied dance at the University of North Carolina, where he majored in drama, wrote for several college publications and worked with the famed Carolina Playmakers. He continued to study dance in all its forms under various teachers in preparation for his career as a dance critic.

Mr. Terry's first assignment as dance critic was with the Boston *Herald* in 1936. From 1939 to 1966 he held the dual post of dance editor and critic for the New York *Herald Tribune,* except for the three years he served in the U.S. Army Air Corps during World War II. Since 1967 Mr. Terry has been dance critic and editor of *Saturday Review.*

In addition to his newspaper work, Mr. Terry has written extensively for such magazines as *Theatre Arts, Dance News, Dance Magazine, Horizon* and *Kenyon Review.* He is also dance editor for the *Encyclopaedia Britannica.* He lectures frequently on coast-to-coast tours of cities, colleges, universities, public schools and clubs.

Mr. Terry's books include *Invitation to the Dance; Star Performance; Ballet in Action* (with Paul Himmel) ; *The Dance in America; Ballet: A New Guide to the Liveliest Art; On Pointe!; Isadora Duncan; The Ballet Companion; Miss Ruth: The "More Living Life" of Ruth St. Denis;* and *Ballet: A Pictorial History.*

73 74 75   12 11 10 9 8 7 6 5 4 3 2 1